Better Homes and Gardens®

handmade greetings
for all occasions

W9-BFE-909

Better Homes and Gardens® Books
Des Moines, Iowa

Better Homes and Gardens® Books
An imprint of Meredith® Books

Handmade Greetings for All Occasions
Editor: Carol Field Dahlstrom
Writer: Susan M. Banker
Designer: Lyne Neymeyer
Copy Chief: Terri Fredrickson
Copy and Production Editor: Victoria Forlini
Editorial Operations Manager: Karen Schirm
Managers, Book Production: Pam Kvitne, Marjorie J. Schenkelberg, Rick von Holdt
Contributing Copy Editor: Margaret Smith
Contributing Proofreaders: Colleen Johnson, Anne Terpstra, Pam Wright
Photographers: Peter Krumhardt, Scott Little, Andy Lyons Cameraworks
Technical Illustrator: Shawn Drafahl
Electronic Production Coordinator: Paula Forest
Editorial and Design Assistants: Kaye Chabot, Mary Lee Gavin, Karen McFadden

Meredith® Books
Publisher and Editor in Chief: Linda Raglan Cunningham
Design Director: Matt Strelecki
Executive Editor, Food and Crafts: Jennifer Dorland Darling

Publisher: James D. Blume
Executive Director, Marketing: Jeffrey Myers
Executive Director, New Business Development: Todd M. Davis
Executive Director, Sales: Ken Zagor
Director, Operations: George A. Susral
Director, Production: Douglas M. Johnston
Business Director: Jim Leonard

Vice President and General Manager: Douglas J. Guendel

Better Homes and Gardens® Magazine
Editor in Chief: Karol DeWulf Nickell

Meredith Publishing Group
President, Publishing Group: Stephen M. Lacy
Vice President-Publishing Director: Bob Mate

Meredith Corporation
Chairman and Chief Executive Officer: William T. Kerr

Chairman of the Executive Committee: E. T. Meredith III

All of us at Better Homes and Gardens® Books are dedicated to providing you with information and ideas to create beautiful and useful projects. We welcome your comments and suggestions. Write to us at: Better Homes and Gardens Books, Crafts Editorial Department, 1716 Locust Street—LN112, Des Moines, IA 50309-3023.

If you would like to purchase any of our crafts, cooking, gardening, home improvement, or home decorating and design books, check wherever quality books are sold. Or visit us at: bhgbooks.com

Permission is given to photocopy the patterns in this book for personal use only.

contents

greetings forever

The tradition of sending greetings is a natural one. We all want to share our thoughts when an occasion arises,

This 1890s angel is a piece of "scrap" that could be bought for pennies at a general store.

but sometimes it is difficult to tell someone how we feel, or it may not be convenient to be somewhere in person. But it is always lovely to write a version of a sentiment just when the time is right. And it is even more lovely when that greeting is handmade.

In this book of handmade greetings we have shared ideas for most every occasion. From birthdays and weddings to favorite

This elegant card was handmade around 1890 from pieces of "scrap" and lacy paper.

holidays and "just because" occasions we've offered ideas for making your own special statement. Many of these cards can be made in just a few minutes, while others require a bit more attention. But whatever cards you choose to make, you can be sure your effort will be appreciated by the person who is lucky enough to receive your handmade greeting.

For years and years making and sending handmade greetings has been a cherished art form. It would be impossible to know when the first lovely thought was written on paper to present to a special person

or when the first kind remark was penned and passed from hand to hand. Some beautiful paper sentiments have been tucked away only to be found years later. Sometimes we know who wrote and designed the lovely greetings that we have found because they are signed and sealed. But sometimes we can only imagine who cared so much to create these lovely works of art to share.

We do know that handmade cards were made in Victorian times using paper "scrap". These tiny pieces of die-cut paper were available for pennies at the general store.

Often cherished by young girls to paste into their scrapbooks, these tiny pieces of colorful paper were also used for delicate card-making. Some of the cards were one-sided greetings and others opened up to reveal golden embellished pieces of paper combined with a variety of "scraps" to create a lovely card. Some were hand painted with cherished water paints while others were written with fine ink pens.

In the early 1900s purchased postcards became available and were common ways to send greetings. Holidays became a wonderful reason to send these colorful purchased cards. They were also sent when someone was lucky enough to travel away from home and share

Felt, feathers, and trims were often added to cards made in the 1960s.

that rare excitement. Sometimes when looking at these purchased postcards from years ago, we can see that the sender added a bit of embellishment to make the card seem more personal —perhaps the addition of their name in glitter.

During the mid 20th century there are many examples of handmade notecards and holiday cards where a simple image was glued in the corner of a note to personalize it or a bit of crochet or quilling was added for interest.

Dated 1910, this postcard shows a glittered signature added by the giver.

Today our array of papers and products for making paper cards has never been more exciting. At our very fingertips we have papers in every color and style, stickers and stamps to fit any scheme, paints and markers to write and color our greetings, and embellishments to make every greeting a piece of art.

We have always wanted to share our warmest sentiments with the people we love. What better time than now to join in the spirit of creating handmade greetings—pieces of art to be cherished forever by the people that you love the most.

Carol Field Dahlstrom

card-making basics

Gather your supplies

Although scrapbooking and crafts stores sell a wide assortment of supplies for cardmaking, if you have these basics, the process is a snap:

- Card stock
- Decorative scrapbook papers
- Paper cutter (see Photos A and B, *right*, for use in cutting and measuring)
- Crafts knife
- Scoring tool
- Ruler, preferably metal
- Pencil
- Mat for work surface protection
- Glue stick
- Spray adhesive
- Scissors and decorative-edge scissors
- Adjustable circle cutter
- Envelopes or large sheets of paper to make envelopes (see *pages 109–110* for tips and patterns)

Additional items to add interest to your cards include buttons, clay, embossing supplies, ribbons and trims, paint, marking and gel pens, stickers, ribbon roses, gems and rhinestones, charms, and photographs. As you make cards for family and friends, remember to personalize them with meaningful embellishments.

Protecting your work surface

Since making cards can involve such supplies as spray adhesive, paint, marking pens, circle cutters, embossing supplies, and crafts knives, here's how to protect yourself and your environment.

Use spray adhesive or spray paint in a well-ventilated work area. Because the mist from these products may scatter, cover the surfaces well with newspapers. Read the product label and wear a mask if recommended.

Use a protective mat when using a crafts knife. These mats, a good investment because they save tables from unsightly nicks and cuts, are self-healing, and can be used for years.

Before using a circle or oval cutter, read the product instructions and protect your work surface. Many cutters come with a glass work sheet to place beneath the paper to be cut (see Photo C, *below right.*)

When using such materials as paint, glue, marking pens, and embossing gel, cover the work surface with newspapers or a plastic tablecloth. Also have paper towels and a damp rag on hand for clean-up and spills.

Using the tools

Some of the basic cardmaking steps are illustrated *right* and *opposite.* While not all of the cards in this book use these methods, you'll find several that do. It is wise to score card stock and other heavyweight papers before folding, to ensure a smooth fold. (For help using a scoring tool, see Photos D–F, *opposite.*) When a card is made with a paper base, no scoring is necessary.

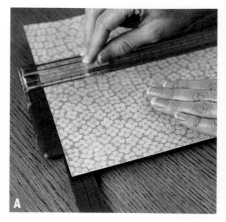

Use a paper trimmer to cut straight lines easily. Many trimmers include a ruler as a helpful guide.

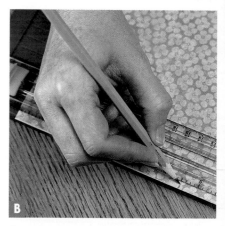

Use the ruler on the paper trimmer to measure and draw straight lines.

Use an adjustable circle cutter to make perfect circles in a variety of sizes.

Use a scoring tool (also called a creasing tool or bone folder) to help create a neat fold. Run the tip of the tool along a ruler to mark the fold.

Use the side of the scoring tool to smooth down the fold.

Hand-press the fold carefully so it is smooth.

When folding paper, it's important to first find the paper grain—the direction in which paper fibers align. Paper folded parallel to the grain produces cleaner folds and lies flatter which is important in cardmaking.

Throughout the book you'll also discover a variety of glues being used. We've listed what our card designers used, however you may substitute your favorite adhesive if it is applicable for a particular technique.

Choosing papers

When looking for papers to make handmade greetings, you will find a huge selection of colors, patterns, weights, and textures available in art, crafts, and scrapbooking stores.

Commonly available specialty papers include vellum, card stock, handmade paper, solid and patterned papers, and paper with metallic finishes. The standard sizes of paper are 4×6, 5×7, $8^1/_2$×11, and 12×12.

Many papers are grouped with coordinating colors and patterns that will lend continuity to a creation. However, feel free to mix and match

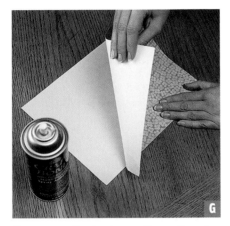

Use spray adhesive in a well-ventilated work area to adhere papers back-to-back creating two-sided pages.

your papers to give your greetings character and make them unique.

You'll find some patterned scrapbook papers are two-sided, displaying a different pattern on each side. To create your own combinations, use spray adhesive to bond papers back to back (see the Photo G, *above*).

To ensure the longevity of your greeting, you should choose materials that are acid-free and lignin-free, or labeled "of archival quality" or "photo safe." Products that are acid-free and lignin-free have a pH factor of 7.0 or above, and do not yellow or damage photographs.

What about the envelope?
You can purchase envelopes at crafts, scrapbooking, and paper and office supply stores in a variety of colors, sizes, and materials. Sometimes it is wise to create a card to fit an envelope rather than the other way around. To make an envelope for your handcrafted cards, see pages 109–110 for tips and patterns for three sizes of envelopes.

special occasions

Many times throughout the year you'll want to send best wishes. Whether honoring a birth or sending a heartfelt thank you, acknowledging a wedding or celebrating a birthday, these handmade greetings will make their way into the hearts of those who are dear to yours.

floral fancy

what you'll need

- 9¹/₄×7 lime green card stock
- White fine iridescent tissue or transparent paper
- Cardboard
- Approximately 2 yards of sheer orange ribbon
- Purple silk flowers; leaves
- Seed beads
- Ruler; pencil; scoring tool
- Paper trimmer
- Tape
- Thick white crafts glue
- Envelope or paper and tracing paper

here's how

1 Measure and mark the fold line on the green card stock. Run a scoring tool, held with very little pressure, along the fold line. Fold the green card stock in half along the score line.

2 Cut a 5¹/₂×3¹/₂-inch rectangle of cardboard. Cut a 6¹/₂×4¹/₂-inch rectangle of tissue paper. Cover the cardboard with white tissue paper; tape the edges of the tissue paper to the back of the cardboard.

3 Tape one end of the orange ribbon to the back side of covered cardboard. Wrap the ribbon around the cardboard, crossing it in the center, and taping it in place on the back side at every wrap.

4 Remove stem, leaves, and any plastic centers from silk flowers. Glue several small silk flowers and a leaf in the center of the ribbon. Glue a cluster of seed beads in the center of each flower.

5 To make an envelope, see *pages 109–110.* Glue a small flower with beaded center on the envelope.

greetings

Best wishes today and always.

Friends are flowers in the garden of life. And you are one of the brightest blooms in my bouquet!

This elegant greeting will plant beautiful thoughts in the heart of any recipient. Pick meaningful silk flowers to personalize the sentiment.

time for tea

Pretty papers pair with shiny gold tea trims to make a lovely invitation. The lace-trimmed flap lifts to reveal party details.

what you'll need

- Victorian-style floral paper
- 5×10 coordinating card stock
- Tracing paper and pencil
- Lace or braid trim
- Gold sticker letters
- Gold tea-themed charms
- Ruler; pencil
- Scoring tool
- Paper trimmer
- Crafts knife or scissors
- Spray adhesive; newspapers
- Thick white crafts glue
- Envelope or paper and tracing paper

here's how

1 Measure and mark a fold line on the card stock. Run a scoring tool, held with very little pressure, along the fold line. Fold the card stock in half along the score line.

2 Cover a work surface in a well-ventilated work area with newspapers. Spray the back side of the floral paper; affix it to the front panel. Use a ruler and pencil to measure and mark the floral flap, the point 1 inch from the bottom of the card. Open card and cut flap with a crafts knife.

3 Glue lace or braid trim around the front panel. Let the glue dry.

4 To determine lettering placement, use a pencil and tracing paper. Trace the flap and lettering area. Draw a base line with pencil and roughly trace the desired sticker letters. Trim this tracing with a straight edge. Tape the card onto a work surface. Tape the tracing over the card just below the letter placement. Use the tracing as a guide and adhere lettering in place as shown in Photo A, *above right*.

5 Glue on tea charms with crafts glue.

6 To make an envelope, see *pages 109–110*. Trim the envelope flap with lace or braid trim.

A

greetings

Join us for tea, cake, and the wonderful conversation of dear friends.

Please come to a tea party on _____ at _____.

sincere thanks

what you'll need

- Coordinating textweight papers and card stock in desired sizes
- Decorator foil, such as 38-gauge Maid-o'-Metal aluminum goldtone foil
- Leaf
- Acrylic glaze paint colors
- Ruler; pencil; scissors
- Pinking shears
- Embossing tool
- Thick crafts foam
- Burnisher

- Paintbrush
- Soft cloth, tissue, or cotton ball
- Paper trimmer
- Glue stick
- Thick white crafts glue
- Envelope or paper and tracing paper
- Gold pen

here's how

1 Measure, mark, and trim foil piece into the desired size. The leaf foil shown is 5×4¹/₄ inches, and the pinked foil is 3¹/₂ inches square. Cut the foil with straight-edge scissors or pinking shears. If desired, roll the corners as on the leaf card.

2 To make designs, use an embossing tool on foil. Place the foil on a thick piece of crafts foam, providing a soft work surface. Write the message and draw a border or other design as shown in Photo A, *left*. To make the leaf, place the leaf on a hard surface, place foil over it, and carefully and firmly rub a burnisher over the image to transfer it.

3 Brush acrylic glaze on the image. Let the glaze partially dry; gently wipe away the color from raised surfaces using a soft cloth, tissue, or cotton ball, as shown in Photo B.

4 To create the card background, measure and mark the fold line on the card stock. Run a scoring tool, held with very little pressure, along the fold line. Fold the card stock in half along the score line. If desired, glue additional colored papers to the background.

5 Use a small amount of crafts glue to affix the foil piece to the card.

6 To make an envelope, see *pages 109–110*. Trim the envelope by gluing small pieces of paper on it or embellishing the flap with gold pen.

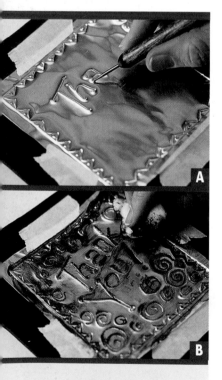

A

B

greeting

You are too, too kind! (But thanks!)

Embed your own handwriting and a pretty motif to send a heartfelt word of thanks. Decorator foil makes the process easy.

what you'll need for all cards

- Card stock in black and colors to coordinate with appliqués
- Adhesive-back stitched animal appliqué
- Ruler; pencil
- Scoring tool
- Paper trimmer
- Glue stick
- Envelope or paper and tracing paper

for bear card

- Colored paper in light brown, dark brown, and black
- Scissors

for giraffe card

- Crafts paper
- Giraffe print rubber stamp (available in scrapbook and stamping stores)
- Copper stamp pad
- Metallic gold marking pen
- Fine-line black marking pen

for tiger card

- Construction paper in orange and black
- Coordinating papers in card stock and textweight in desired sizes
- Soft cloth, tissue, or cotton ball
- Paper trimmer; glue stick
- Thick white crafts glue
- Gold pen

here's how

1 Measure and mark the fold line on the card stock. Run a scoring tool, held with very little pressure, along the fold line. Fold the card stock in half along the score line.

2 Using the photograph for inspiration, cut paper layers to enhance the background. Use a glue stick to affix in place.

3 *For the bear card,* cut two 1¹/₂×5-inch strips from each of the three colored papers. Working with a set of three strips at a time, use scissors to cut an irregular sawtooth edge along one long side. Repeat with the remaining three paper strips. Arrange the strips, black at the bottom, dark brown, and light brown, reversing every other strip. To appear as fur, glue in place on card front. Peel off paper backing from the bear appliqué; press in place.

4 *For the giraffe card,* stamp the crafts paper with the giraffe-print rubber stamp. Let dry. Tear a square to fit the front of the card and a strip for the bottom of the card. Glue the pieces in place. Peel off paper backing from giraffe appliqué and press in place. Use a gold marking pen to make sets of short lines to accent the background paper edge. Write a message in gold. Shade the left side of each letter using black pen.

5 *For the tiger card,* tear strips and Vs from black construction paper. Arrange the black pieces on orange construction paper to resemble a tiger coat. Glue the pieces in place. Trim the paper to fit the front of the card. Glue in place. Peel off the paper backing from the tiger appliqué and press onto contrasting paper. Layer papers if desired. Glue the tiger to the lefthand corner of the card.

6 To make an envelope, see *pages 109–110.*

Made with a brawny touch, the purchased
appliqués on these greeting cards are enhanced
with stamped, torn, and cut-paper backgrounds.

purse note cards

Fun scrapbook papers cut in mini purse shapes send fashionable statements. The handles, attached with brad paper fasteners, make these cute cards resemble real totes.

what you'll need

- Heavyweight solid and patterned scrapbook paper
- Colored vellum
- Tracing paper
- Mini brad paper fasteners
- Pencil
- Scissors
- Crafts knife; glue stick
- $3/4$- and $5/8$-inch hole punches
- Adhesive hook and loop fasteners, such as Velcro
- Envelope or paper and tracing paper

here's how

1 Trace the patterns, *opposite;* cut out the shapes.

2 Fold both the patterned paper and vellum sheet in half. Place the pattern against the fold line and trace the purse shape onto each piece. Cut out the purse shape from both papers. Use the pattern to cut two handles from solid paper.

3 Open the patterned paper purse and position the handle ends at the top of the purse. Use a crafts knife to cut slits through the handle ends and purse (as indicated by the dots on the purse handle pattern). Thread mini brads through the slits;

separate the metal ends on the inside of the card.

4 Use the pattern to cut the closure strip from solid paper. Fold it on the line indicated. Glue one end to the inside back of the purse. Glue two punched or handcut circles (patterns, *below*) to the other end of the paper strip. Press one half of the hook and loop fastener under the circle and the other half to the front of the purse. Glue the vellum purse inside the finished patterned paper purse. Glue a contrasting paper shape inside card, if desired.

5 To make an envelope, see *pages 109–110.*

Fold
Purse Pattern

Purse Handle Pattern

Cut 2

½"

1"

Purse Closure Patterns

2¾"

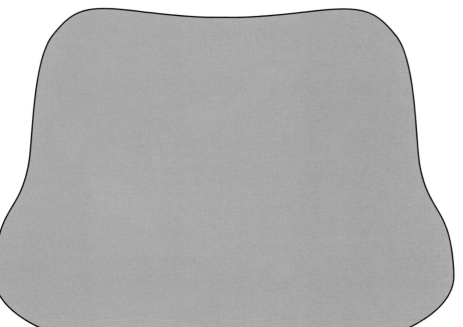

...a Penny for your thoughts...

for the happy couple

Glitter sparkles at the edges of the pretty stamped design and pastel papers add softness to this intricate greeting.

what you'll need

- Card stock in pink and white
- Pink and white translucent papers
- White glitter
- Ruler; pencil
- Rubber stamp dove or other design
- Embossing ink pad
- Embossing powder
- Heat gun; paper trimmer; scoring tool
- Glue stick; glue pen
- Envelope or paper and tracing paper

here's how

1 Using a well-inked stamp, press the stamp onto the translucent white paper. Quickly sprinkle embossing powder over stamped image. Shake off the excess powder.

2 Use the heat gun to heat the stamped image until it becomes opaque and raised.

3 Tear the edge around the stamped image. Tear a pink layer of paper. Use a glue pen around edges and sprinkle with white glitter. Shake off the excess.

4 Measure and mark the fold line on the pink card stock. Run a scoring tool, held with very little pressure, along the fold line. Fold the card stock in half along the score line.

5 Trim a piece of white card stock smaller than the pink panel and glue to the pink panel with a glue stick. Layer the torn pink and embossed papers and glue to the card center.

6 To make an envelope, see *pages 109–110*.

greetings

May your wedding day be bright and beautiful as you say "I do."

With friendship and love, we celebrate your wedding day.

You make a perfect pair.

Enjoy your wedding day as the two of you become one.

the gown

A traditional symbol, this miniature lace gown adorns the front of a card that can be used for a shower or wedding. This card uses purple and lavender, but you can choose any hue to suit the wedding party's color scheme.

what you'll need

- 10×6¾ light lavender scrapbook paper
- Purple self-stick vellum
- Wedding dress sticker, such as Jolee's Boutique
- Rhinestone adhesive letters
- Ruler; pencil
- Decorative-edge scissors
- Envelope or paper and tracing paper

here's how

1. Measure and mark the fold line on the lavender paper. Fold the paper in half.
2. Using decorative scissors, cut the purple vellum 4½×2½ inches. Center and stick it to the card.
3. Remove the rhinestone letters to spell "love" and press on the card at the bottom center. Place the dress sticker in the center of the vellum.
4. If you wish to make an envelope, see *pages 109–110*. To trim the envelope flap cut a strip from purple vellum. Trim one edge with decorative-edge scissors. Press onto the edge of the envelope flap.
5. **For the tag,** cut the background paper the desired size. Trim with a contrasting strip at the top, cut with decorative-edge scissors. Using the photo, *left,* as a guide, cut a small paper bow from coordinating papers. Glue papers in place. Punch a hole in the corner.

greetings

All you need is love.

Happy bride and groom day!

Congratulations to our friends, the new Mr. and Mrs. (personalized name here).

wedding day wonders

greetings

Now you may kiss the bride!

May all your days be the happily-ever-after kind.

what you'll need

- Pencil; ruler; scoring tool
- Envelopes or paper and tracing paper

for the tuxedo

- 11×5½ white card stock; 4¼×4⅞ silver paper
- Black and white striped scrapbook paper
- Black and silver striped scrapbook paper
- 2-inch squares of white tissue paper
- Paper scraps in red and white; ⅛-inch-wide red satin ribbon; ⅛-inch hole punch

for the veil

- 11×5½ white card stock
- 4⅛×4¾ pearlized patterned paper
- Small wedding flowers with pearls
- Four 4½×5 pieces of white tulle
- Small safety pin; hot-glue gun; glue sticks

here's how

1 For either card, measure and mark the fold line on the card stock. Run a scoring tool, held with very little pressure, along the fold line. Fold the card stock in half.

2 To make the tuxedo card, glue silver paper to the center of the card front. Trace the pattern, *below;* cut out. Use pattern to cut tuxedo from black and silver stripe paper. Punch one hole in each cuff and punch three buttonholes down the center. Glue red paper scraps behind the holes for buttons. Cut out the lapels from black and white stripe paper; glue to jacket front. Make three ⅛-inch pleats down the center of the tissue paper. Center the pleats along the tuxedo jacket, gluing the tissue edges under the jacket. Trim excess tissue paper. Cut out collar from white paper; glue it to the top of the shirt. Tie a small red ribbon bow, trim the ends, and glue it below collar. Center and glue the tuxedo to the card.

3 To make the veil card, glue pearlized paper to the center of the card front. Stack four layers of tulle and thread the safety pin through one edge. Hot-glue four or five small wedding flowers over the safety pin, aligning the strings of pearls on the sides of the veil. Hot-glue the veil to the pearlized paper.

4 To make an envelope, see *pages 109–110.* To embellish the envelope, glue one of the specialty papers to the flap.

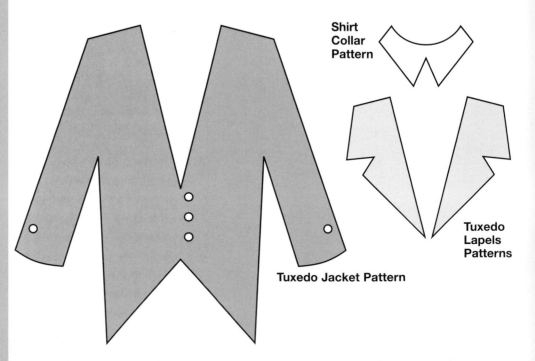

Shirt Collar Pattern

Tuxedo Lapels Patterns

Tuxedo Jacket Pattern

baby cards

Welcome a newborn with a keepsake card made with paper, felt, and rickrack. Any card from this charming trio is sure to make it into baby's scrapbook.

what you'll need
- Purchased white note cards and envelopes
- White baby rickrack; white stiffened felt
- Thick white crafts glue; glue stick

for the booties card
- Yellow patterned scrapbook paper
- Yellow baby rickrack
- White satin ribbon rose and bow

for the diaper card
- Blue patterned scrapbook paper
- 2 small silver safety pins; blue baby rickrack

for the baby card
- Pink patterned scrapbook paper
- Flesh color paper
- Pink and flesh color pencils; doll hair
- White satin ribbon rose and bow
- Pink baby rickrack; fine black marking pen

here's how

1 Cut scrapbook paper the same size as the note card. Trim $1^1/_2$ inches from the long edge. Fold it in half, short ends together. Center and glue the paper to note card. Glue rickrack along edges of patterned paper.

2 For the diaper, cut both diaper pieces from white felt. Glue the small diaper front over the larger diaper back, aligning bottom edges. Fold and pin the diaper back sides over the front. Use crafts glue to attach blue rickrack across the top edge of the diaper front. Mount the diaper to the center of the prepared card.

greetings

Welcome to the world little one!

Sending our best wishes to the entire family.

Wishing you... glee-filled days... some sleep at night... and moment after moment of wonderful firsts.

3 *For the baby,* cut the swaddled baby shape from white felt. Trace the head opening onto colored paper. With the fine marking pen, draw two sets of eyelashes, a small nose, and tiny lips on the head. Add color to the baby's face with the pink and flesh color pencils. Glue the head to the back side of the felt, face showing through opening. Thread one end of a small lock of doll hair between the felt and colored paper at the top of the baby's head. Use crafts glue to attach the pink rickrack along front of swaddled baby and a satin rose and bow under the baby's chin. Glue baby to card.

4 *For the booties,* cut a pair of booties from felt. Glue yellow baby rickrack and a ribbon rose and bow to the top of each bootie. Glue finished booties on the prepared card.

5 To make an envelope, see *pages 109–110.*

Bootee Patterns

Diaper Front Pattern

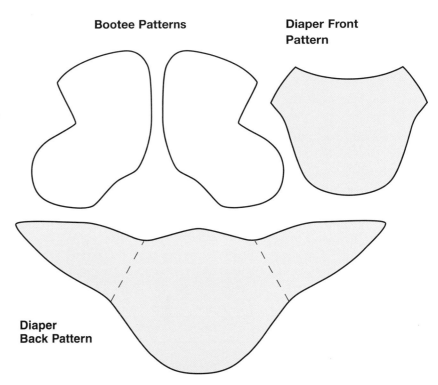

Diaper Back Pattern

Baby Blanket Pattern

whimsical and wacky cheer-up card

what you'll need

- 8¹/₂×7 patterned turquoise and purple background paper
- 3¹/₄×6¹/₄ yellow card stock
- 3¹/₂×6¹/₂ purple card stock; colored wire
- Star eyelets
- Large white button
- Large seed beads; sticker letters
- Ruler; pencil; scoring tool
- Pinking shears
- Circle template
- Paper punch tool; hammer; eyelet tool
- Thin handled paintbrush; glue stick
- Thick white crafts glue
- Envelope or paper and tracing paper

here's how

1 Measure and mark the fold line on the background paper. Run a scoring tool, held with very little pressure, along the fold line. Fold the card stock in half along the score line.

2 Trim yellow card stock with pinking shears. On the back, mark a half circle using a circle template. Mark five points on the half circle for eyelets. Punch holes at each mark using a punch and hammer, as shown in Photo A, *below left.* Place eyelets in holes, tops on the front of paper. Turn over and pound back side of eyelets with tool and hammer, as shown in Photo B

3 Cut colored wires into 9-inch lengths. Insert wires through two of the eyelets and coil the ends around a paintbrush handle to resemble hair, as shown in Photo C. Flatten the wire on the back of the card.

4 Layer and adhere the yellow paper to the purple paper, then to the card front.

5 Use crafts glue to glue a button below the eyelets. Glue on beads for a face.

6 Adhere letter stickers to colored paper for a message. Glue in place.

7 To make an envelope, see *pages 109–110.* Accent envelope with cut pieces of paper.

A

B

C

Coils of colored wire sprouting from star-shape eyelets along with a bead and button face make this card a real cheerer-upper!

BAD DAY?
CHEER UP!

blooming best wishes

Whatever the special occasion, this dainty design bursts with best wishes.

what you'll need

- 10×5¼ metallic gold card stock
- 4½×4¾ peach paper
- 4⅛-inch square of white paper
- Scraps of colored paper or vellum
- Ruler; pencil; scoring tool; paper punch
- Scissors; decorative-edge scissors
- Fine-line metallic gold marking pen
- Glue stick
- Envelope or paper and tracing paper

here's how

1 On gold card stock, measure and mark the fold line. Run a scoring tool, held with very little pressure, along the fold line. Fold the card stock in half along the score line.

2 Center and glue the peach paper on the card front. Glue white paper on the peach paper.

3 From paper or vellum scraps, make three flowers, cutting circles and ovals. For dots, use a paper punch.

4 Use a glue stick to adhere layered pieces and to apply flowers to the card front.

5 Draw stems, leaves, and flower and envelope accents using a gold pen. To make an envelope, see *pages 109–110*.

6 For the tag, cut out a paper background. Cut a smaller piece from contrasting paper using decorative-edge scissors; center and glue to background paper. Cut out a simple flower shape from colorful papers. Glue on card. Draw stem and leaves with a marking pen. Punch a hole in one corner.

greetings
*... today
and always.*

*No matter where
you are, you are in
my heart.*

polka-dot pals

Use paper punches in a variety of sizes to accent a trio of favorite animal shapes.

materials for all cards

- Tracing paper
- Pencil
- Scissors
- Three sizes of hole punches
- Glue stick

for the dog card

- 9×7³/₄ heavy black paper
- 9×1 black and white dotted paper
- 9×4 and 7×4 white paper
- Scraps of paper in red and black
- Red business-size envelope

for the giraffe card

- 9×7³/₄ heavy orange paper
- 9×4 orange and white dotted paper

- 9×4 yellow paper
- Scraps of orange and black papers
- Fine-line black marking pen
- Yellow business-size envelope

for the frog card

- 9×7³/₄ heavy, medium green paper
- 9×4 green striped paper
- 7×4 light green paper
- Black paper scrap
- Green business-size envelope
- 3¹/₂-inch square of light green paper
- 3¹/₄×8³/₄ green striped scrapbook paper
- Black paper scrap

here's how

1 Fold the background paper (black for the dog, medium green for the frog, and orange for the giraffe) in half, short ends together. Glue the patterned paper inside the card. For the dog card, glue the white paper inside the card, adding the dotted strip on the bottom edge.

2 Trace the desired pattern, *pages 28–29*. Cut out and trace around patterns on colored papers. Cut out the dog body from white paper, the dog's ear and nose from black paper, and his bow from red paper. Cut the frog pattern from light green paper, the giraffe body pattern from yellow paper, the top of the tail and ear from orange paper, and the tail end and eye from black paper.

3 Punch the cut pattern shapes with the three different size hole punches. Arrange and glue an animal on the card cover.

4 For the frog, punch eyes using two standard-size holes from black paper scrap; glue in place. Use the fine marker to draw the giraffe's mouth.

5 For the envelopes, punch a variety of holes in the envelope corners so that the contrasting color card will appear through the openings. For the frog envelope, glue a striped-paper rectangle in the center of the envelope. Adhere a partial frog just left of center.

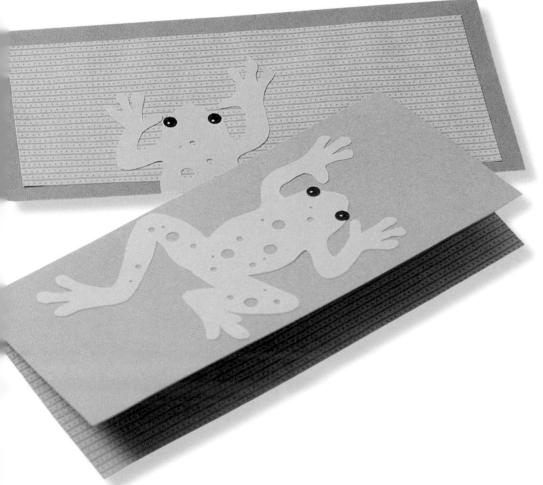

greetings

Doggone! How can you have a birthday when you don't look any older??
(for the dog card)

❧

I'm stretching my neck out here, but isn't it your birthday?
(for the giraffe card)

❧

Hop to it and have a great birthday!
(for the frog card)

❧

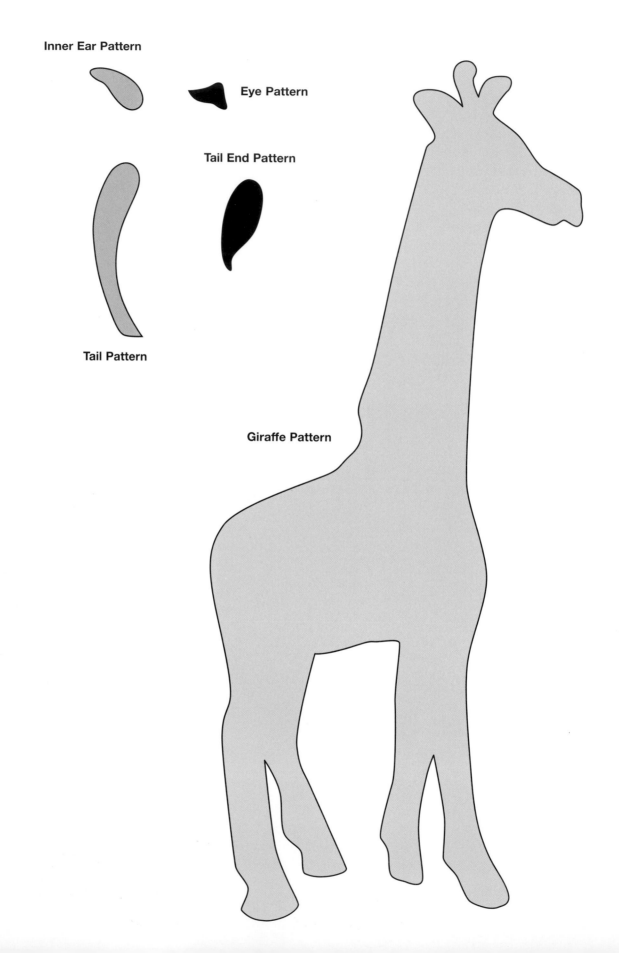

Inner Ear Pattern

Eye Pattern

Tail End Pattern

Tail Pattern

Giraffe Pattern

28

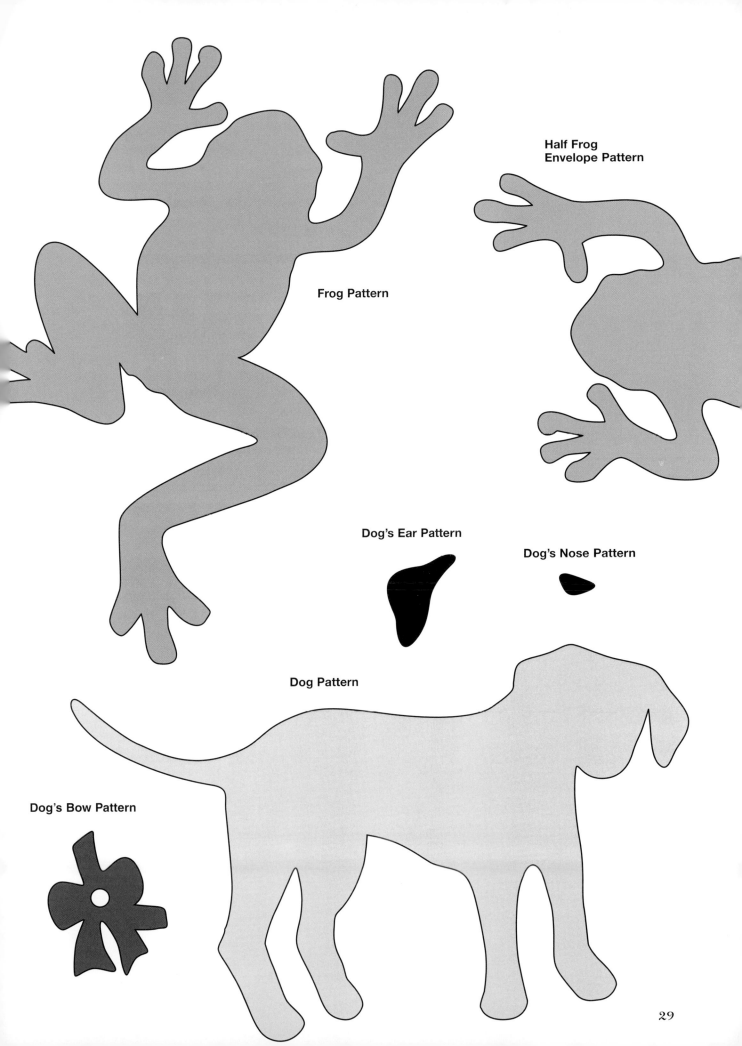

**Half Frog
Envelope Pattern**

Frog Pattern

Dog's Ear Pattern

Dog's Nose Pattern

Dog Pattern

Dog's Bow Pattern

29

birthday bubbles

what you'll need

- 6×12 white card stock
- 4³/₄-inch square of black paper
- Paper in lime green and turquoise
- ¹/₄-inch-high press-on white vinyl lettering
- Ruler; pencil; scoring tool
- Circle cutter; glue stick
- Envelope or paper and tracing paper

here's how

1 Measure and mark the fold line on the card stock. Run a scoring tool, held with very little pressure, along the fold line. Fold the card stock in half along the score line. Glue the black paper in the card center.

2 Using a circle cutter, cut two 3-inch circles from turquoise paper and one from lime green paper. Using the photo, *below*, as a guide, arrange, trim, and glue on the circles.

3 Adhere HAPPY BIRTHDAY lettering across the full circle on the card front, aligning the initial letters of each word.

4 To make an envelope, see *pages 109–110*. To trim the envelope, glue coordinating paper strips on the flap.

5 **For the tag,** cut out four graduated-size paper circles. Glue the three smaller circles together; layer on large circle. Punch a hole near one edge; secure with an eyelet. Press adhesive letters on front. Slide circles apart to write a message inside.

greetings
In our circle of friends, you're one of our favorites!

Enjoy this day... it's all yours!

bright birthday wishes

Glistening sequins dance around the border of this birthday greeting and dazzling press-on lettering conveys happy wishes.

what you'll need

- Card stock in white, purple, and yellow or other desired colors
- Colored sticker letters; multicolor sequins
- Tracing paper; ruler; pencil
- Paper trimmer; scoring tool
- Decorative-edge scissors; glue stick
- Thick white crafts glue
- Envelope or paper and tracing paper

here's how

1 Trim the purple card stock to 5×8 inches. Measure and mark the fold line on the card stock. Run a scoring tool, held with very little pressure, along the fold line. Fold the purple card stock in half along the score line. Using decorative-edge scissors, trim the bottom edge of the card.

2 Cut a 4×3 rectangle from yellow card stock and a 3¼×2 rectangle from white. Layer and glue on the center of the card front.

3 To determine the placement on the white panel, use a pencil and tracing paper to trace the letter sheet for a greeting. Tape the card on a work surface; tape the tracing paper over the card just below positioning. Using the tracing as a guide, press the letters onto the white paper.

4 Apply a wide border of crafts glue around the yellow paper. Sprinkle with sequins. Let dry.

5 To make an envelope, see *pages 109–110*. Glue sequins on the envelope.

6 **For the tag,** cut a rectangle from background paper. Tear or trim the bottom edge with decorative-edge scissors. Cut and glue contrasting paper in the center. Glue sequins around the tag edge. Punch two holes near the top. Apply adhesive lettering to the front of tag.

greeting
*I hope your
birthday sparkles!*

pet-lovers' greetings

Suitable for everyone who loves bow-wows and meows, this adorable pair will add a playful touch to any day.

what you'll need

- 12×6 card stock; scrap of paper
- 5-inch-square piece of contrasting card stock
- 2 sheets of tan heavy adhesive-back felt (available in home centers with furniture pads)
- Small and medium black buttons
- White thread and sewing needle
- Black crafts wire; 1½-inch plastic ring
- Three black pipe cleaners
- ½-inch-wide grosgrain ribbon in the background paper color
- Tracing paper; pencil; scissors; scoring tool
- Glue stick; thick white crafts glue
- Envelope or paper and tracing paper

here's how

1 Trace cat or dog patterns, *opposite,* onto tracing paper. Cut out shapes.
2 With the right side of the pattern pieces on the backing side of the felt, trace around patterns. Cut out the felt shapes.
3 Measure and mark the fold line on the background card stock. Run a scoring tool, held with very little pressure, along the fold line. Fold the card stock in half. Center and glue contrasting paper square to card front.
4 Peel off paper backing from cat or dog face felt piece; press on the card. Apply the ears. For dog, press paper on the adhesive area of the felt ears that extend beyond the card. Trim paper around the ears.

greetings
Wow and meow! Congratulations on your new kitty-cat!

All your best friends wish you a happy birthday!

5 To make the ring around the dog eye, wrap pipe cleaners around a plastic ring. Use crafts glue to adhere it on one side of the dog's face. For cat whiskers, cut three 5-inch-long pieces of wire; thread through shank of button for nose. Twist the wire once on the back to secure. Glue on the button nose.

6 For buttons with holes (non-shank) sew white thread through the holes. Glue the shank button eyes in place.

7 Tie a ribbon bow. Trim the ends. Glue the bow to one side of the dog or cat. Let the glue dry. To make an envelope, see *pages 109–110.*

8 **For the tag,** cut a paper background. Cut a smaller contrasting paper piece; glue in center of tag. Punch a hole in the top and add an eyelet. Glue paper punches to each corner. Cut a triangle from adhesive-back felt; round the top for the mouse head. Sew on two beads for eyes. Cut two felt ears. Sew 4 plies of black thread

through the tip of the nose; knot and trim ends. Remove backing from felt pieces and press in place. Glue a small ribbon bow by one ear. Thread ribbon through the hole.

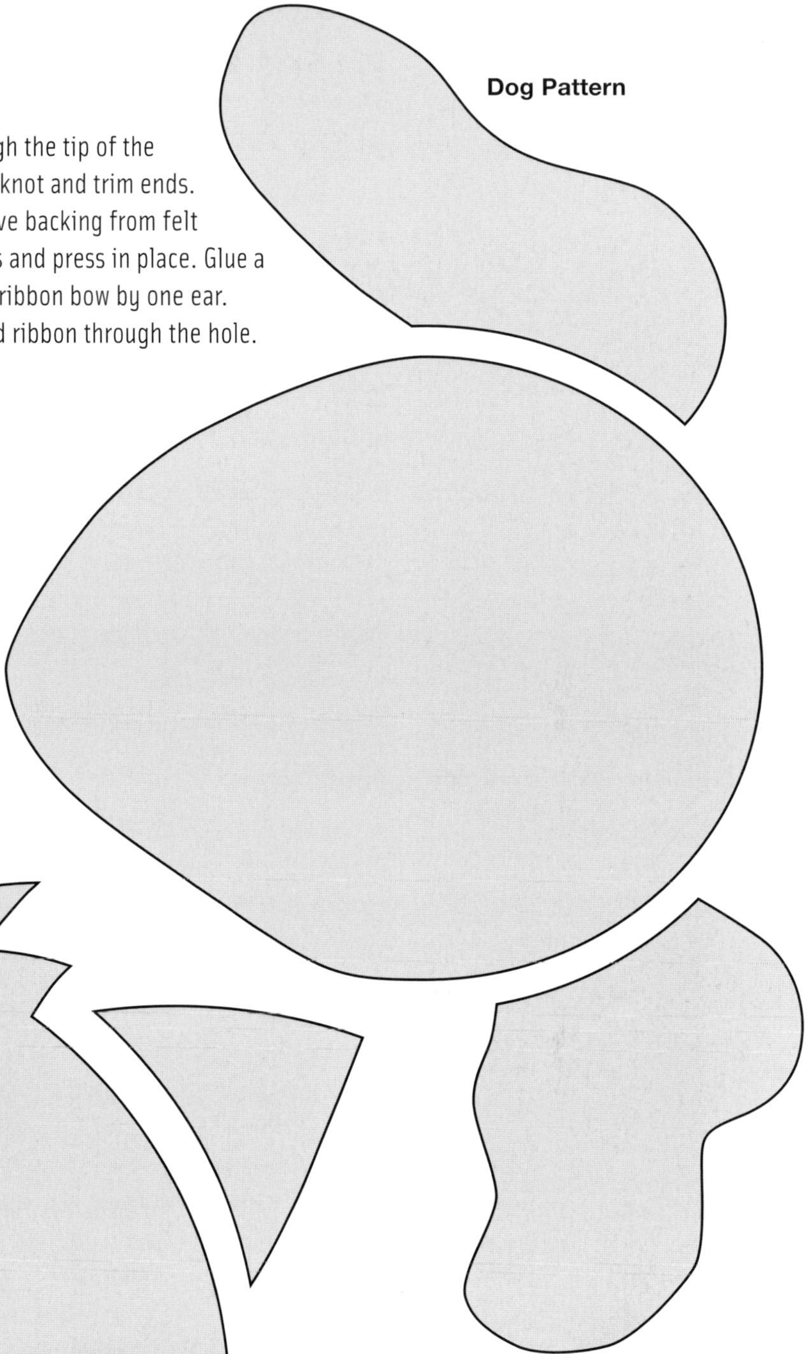

Dog Pattern

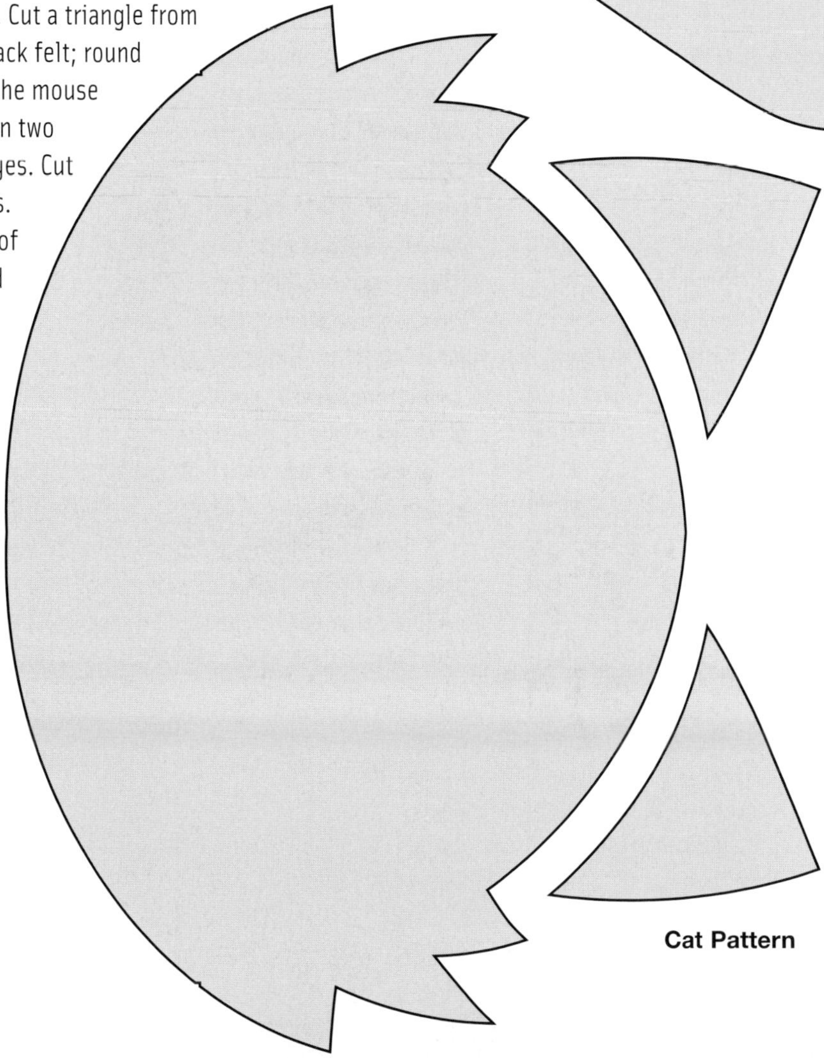

Cat Pattern

wildlife sketches

greetings

May your birthday be naturally beautiful.

To my outdoors guy— happy day!

what you'll need

- Assorted papers and card stock
- Assorted Polyshrink sheets in black, translucent, or clear
- Decorator foil, such as 38-gauge Maid-o'-Metal gold
- Corn husks or raffia
- Pencil; ruler
- Very fine sandpaper; embossing heat gun
- Fine black ink technical pen, soft lead pencil, colored pencil, ballpoint pen, and gold marking pen
- Paper trimmer; scissors; glue stick
- Thick white crafts glue
- Envelope or paper and tracing paper

here's how

1 Sand the Polyshrink material according to product instructions. Polyshrink comes in black (see the Happy Birthday card), translucent (used for the fish and duck), clear, and white. You can use many mediums on the Polyshrink material, such as soft black lead pencil on the duck, technical ink pen on the deer, marker on the gold Happy Birthday, and colored pencil and ballpoint pen on the fish.

2 Photocopy the desired design, *pages 36–37*. Because the plastic will shrink, the final size will be about 45 percent of the pattern in the book.

3 Tape the photocopied pattern onto a flat work surface. Trim the Polyshrink material to the size of the pattern. Tape the Polyshrink piece on the pattern.

4 Trace the pattern lines as neatly as possible, using a very fine black ink technical pen to trace the lines for the deer, or three shades of lead pencil for the duck. First trace all the darkest lines. Fill in the lightest areas, as on the body portion of the duck (see Photo A, *opposite*), and finally fill in the medium tones as on the side of duck face. To color the fish, lightly color it with green pencil.

The color will intensify a little when shrunk. Outline the design with a technical or ballpoint pen.

5 Using an embossing heat gun, heat the drawing approximately 2 inches from the surface (Photo B) to shrink it. It will rapidly curl and distort. You can stop and start any time. If the plastic curls up and touches itself, quickly stop and unbend it, repeating this process as necessary. The plastic will break if you allow it to cool, so move quickly to keep it pliable. Heat until the plastic lies flat again and will shrink no more. While still hot, quickly lay a clean sheet of paper and weight over the plastic for a few seconds to smooth it evenly.

6 To frame a piece of plastic, as shown on the fish, cut a piece of gold foil approximately $3/16$ inch larger all around than the plastic. Lay the plastic on the foil and fold the edges over the plastic.

7 Prepare cards with various layers of coordinating papers. Trim card stock to desired size with paper trimmer. Measure, mark, and score the fold line. Run a scoring tool, held with very little pressure, along fold line. Fold paper in half.

8 Different textures and weights add interest to paper layers. The wavy grass lines on the fish card are cut from the same green card stock and layered onto the card. The cattails on the duck card are cut from velour paper. The plastic pieces may not shrink perfectly square, so trim the frame pieces to coordinate. If desired, glue clear plastic onto the card surface and trim with corn husk strips.

9 To make an envelope, see *pages 109–110*.

A

B

Fish Pattern

Duck Pattern

Permission is granted to photocopy patterns for personal use only.

all-dolled-up-for-you card

what you'll need

- 5×11 white card stock
- 1 sheet patterned paper, such as pink plaid
- 1½-inch square card stock to match plaid color
- 1¼-inch square white card stock
- Small scrap of white vellum
- 5-inch square paper doily
- 3 small buttons (matching plaid paper)
- Flower rubber stamp
- Fine-point black marking pen and various colors
- Black dye-based ink pad
- Ruler; pencil
- Scissors
- Thick white crafts glue
- Envelope or paper and tracing paper

here's how

1 To make the blouse collar, measure down 1⅛ inches from the top of one short end of card stock. At this point make a 1-inch-long cut into the 11-inch side toward the center on each side, as shown on the diagram, *below left*.

2 Mark the card center between the two cuts. Fold collar points to center point; crease.

3 Round the two bottom corners of the collar. Place a small amount of glue under each collar near the top to hold in place. Do not glue down the rounded corners because they will be used to hold the card closed.

4 Fold the bottom of the card up under the collar and even with the back. Round the shoulder corners. Cut and glue pink plaid paper to the front of the blouse and to the inside of collar. Trim any excess.

5 Cut a doily in half diagonally. Center the doily on the card front and glue in place; trim excess doily from edges.

6 Glue buttons on the doily center.

7 Cut a small pocket from pink plaid paper. With black marking pen, draw the stitching lines.

8 Stamp flowers onto vellum with black dye ink. Color the flowers with colored markers. Cut out around the flowers. Glue the flowers to the pocket, then glue pocket to blouse, matching plaid. Write "for you" on the small white card. Center and glue it to the slightly larger square and glue to front of blouse. Let the glue dry. To make an envelope, see *pages 109–110*.

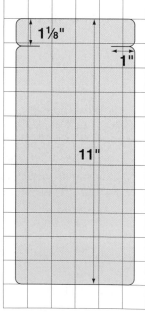

1⅛"

1"

11"

1 square = 1 inch
Reproduce at 400%

seashell sentiments

Say "Happy Mother's Day" with flowers that will last for ages. With just a few simple steps you can create this elegant from-the-sea note.

what you'll need

- 5¼×8½ card stock in desired color
- Coordinating floral paper
- 4 small shells
- White iridescent paint
- Large pearl bead
- Ribbon
- Newspapers
- Paintbrush
- Scoring tool; corner rounder; spray adhesive
- Thick white crafts glue
- Envelope or paper and tracing paper

here's how

1 In a well-ventilated work area, cover work surface with newspapers. Spray adhesive evenly onto the back side of floral paper. Carefully align corners of floral paper and card stock and affix the two together.

2 Measure and mark the fold line on the card stock. Run a scoring tool, held with very little pressure, along the fold line. Fold the card stock in half along the score line.

3 Use a corner rounder on the front panel.

4 Paint the shells iridescent white. Let dry. Use crafts glue to adhere shells in a flower formation. Glue a pearl in the center.

5 Tie a ribbon bow. Glue the bow to the card front, opposite the shell flower.

6 To make an envelope, see *pages 109–110*. Glue a strip of floral paper to the envelope flap.

7 **For the tag,** cut a background from paper. Cut a smaller piece from contrasting paper; center and glue on background. Glue a shell and pearl embellishment to one corner. Punch a hole in the opposite corner. Write a message with tube-style paint. Let dry.

what you'll need

- 8×10¹/₂ antiqued gold card stock
- 5×7³/₄ shiny gold card stock
- Clear gel medium, such as Liquid Crystal (available in scrapbook stores)
- Dyes or inks or transparent waterbase paints in burgundy, green, and rust
- Assorted fibers and decorative trim
- Olive green oven-bake clay, such as Sculpey
- Copper or other desired color of rub-on color accent, such as Rub 'n' Buff
- Buttons and bead; photo
- Rolling tool; frame stamp
- Glass baking dish and oven
- Paintbrush
- Comb
- Black marking pen
- Tape
- Glue stick
- Thick white crafts glue
- Envelope or paper and tracing paper

greetings

Happy Mother's Day to the best grandma I could ever wish for.

⌒⌒

Thank you for making my world a beautiful place...I love you for it.

⌒⌒

here's how

1 Measure and mark the fold line on the antiqued gold card stock. Run a scoring tool, held with very little pressure, along the fold line. Fold the card stock in half along the score line.

2 To accent shiny gold background, randomly spread on the gel medium and several dots of the colored inks. Gently blend the inks with a paintbrush as shown in Photo A, *below,* being careful to not overblend. Let the gel medium begin to dry. As it firms, run a comb through it to create texture, as shown in Photo B, until the desired effect is achieved. Let the gel dry until firm.

3 Wrap strands of various fibers around gold card stock vertically and horizontally; tape in place on the back side. Use a glue stick to attach the gold fibered piece to the card front.

4 Roll out green clay to approximately ¹/₈-inch thickness. Firmly press the frame stamp into the clay to leave a distinct imprint, as shown in Photo C. Trim the inside area with a crafts knife. Tear off the edges as desired. Place clay on a glass baking dish; bake in oven according to product instructions. Remove and let cool.

5 Gently rub on copper color over raised areas on frame, as shown in Photo D. Let dry.

6 Tie strands of fibers around buttons.

7 Handwrite a message on coordinating torn textweight paper and affix with glue stick.

8 Affix a photo under frame with a glue stick. Use crafts glue to attach frame, fibers, and buttons. Tie strands of fibers around folded edge, adding a bead before knotting fiber ends.

9 To make an envelope, see *pages 109–110.* Glue a fiber bow onto envelope flap.

An elegantly framed photo, accompanied by a handwritten sentiment, will pull at any dear grandma's heartstrings.

Grandma, I'll love you always. Anne Mae

especially for you

Shape a school of swimming clay fish on a card that will never be forgotten. Painted with metallic paints, these shimmering fish are pretty enough to frame.

what you'll need

- Coordinating textweight papers and black shiny card stock in desired sizes
- Black oven-bake clay, such as Sculpey
- Acrylic metallic paints, such as Createx
- Rolling tool
- Tracing paper; pencil; scissors; crafts knife
- Small diamond-shape cookie cutter for small fish
- Ink pen with retractable cartridge; drywall screw
- Oven and glass baking dish
- Fine flat paintbrush
- Paper trimmer; pinking shears
- Black marking pen; opaque marking pens in white and green
- Glue stick; thick white crafts glue
- Envelope or paper and tracing paper

here's how

1 On a protected work surface, use a rolling tool to flatten black clay to approximately $1/8$ inch thickness.

2 Trace the desired fish patterns on tracing paper, cut out, and lay on clay. Cut around pattern with crafts knife. Cut out side fins separately. Create different textures using tools. Texture scales using a drywall screw as shown in Photo A, *left*. Make circles with a ballpoint pen with cartridge retracted. Make small dots and lines with a pencil.

3 After the fish body is textured, place side fins. Form small balls for eyes and a long piece for the mouths; press into place. Lay fish in a glass baking dish; bake according to clay product instructions. Let cool.

4 Using very little paint and an almost dry brush, lightly paint the surfaces of the fish,

as shown in Photo B, keeping the paint from seeping into crevices. Blend turquoise into green, orange into red, and pink into purple. To blend colors, such as turquoise and green, begin at one end, painting turquoise downward fading toward center. Paint green from the other direction, fading where the colors overlap. Let dry.

5 Cut card stock for background. Score fold; fold in half. If desired, add paper layers or strips cut with pinking shears. Glue to the background using a glue stick. Use crafts glue to adhere fish. Let dry.

6 To write on black glossy paper, use a white opaque marker first. Let it dry and write over it with a green opaque marker. Use a black marker on lighter colored paper.

7 To make an envelope, see *pages 109–110*. Add strips of coordinating paper to the envelope flap.

Small Fish Pattern

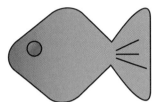

Large Fish Pattern

greetings

You are a one-of-a-kind friend to lucky ol' me.

*I caught you!
(Can I keep you?)*

*Two are always better than one!
Congratulations!*

Medium Fish Pattern

43

pop-up pretties

These little cards are filled with good wishes and fun surprises—dimensional pop-ups that almost sing, "Happy Birthday to You!"

what you'll need

- $5^1/_2 \times 8^1/_2$ colored paper sheet for each card base
- Colored card stock; glue stick
- Envelope or paper and tracing paper

for the cake

- Green paper
- Patterned sticker sheets in light and dark pink, orange, and yellow
- Crafts knife
- Tape

for the present

- Pink and green patterned sticker sheet
- Hole punch

greeting
Here's hoping your birthday is popping with fun!

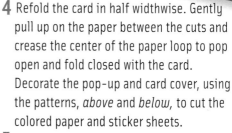

here's how

1 Fold the white paper in half lengthwise and widthwise; crease each fold line. Unfold, showing an X crease through the center of the paper. To cut the pop-up, refold the paper lengthwise. You'll cut the pop-up on the lower half (below the center crease) of the elongated rectangle; the top half will fold down the back to cover the cut opening. Starting at the folded edge, make two 1-inch-long cuts through both paper layers $2^1/_4$ inches apart (1 inch up from the bottom edge and 1 inch down from the crease); unfold the card.

2 *For the present,* lengthen the end of the cuts on one side of the card by $^1/_2$ inch to make a larger present.

3 *For the cake,* use the crafts knife to make two $^1/_8$-inch slits on one side of the cut tab. Insert two candle ends into the openings and tape them in place on the underside of the pop-up. The remaining three candle ends will be trapped between the front of the pop-up cake and the sticker sheet when decorated.

4 Refold the card in half widthwise. Gently pull up on the paper between the cuts and crease the center of the paper loop to pop open and fold closed with the card. Decorate the pop-up and card cover, using the patterns, *above* and *below,* to cut the colored paper and sticker sheets.

5 To make an envelope, see *pages 109–110.* Cut 1-inch-wide strips from sticker sheets to adhere along the bottom edge of the envelopes.

Large Bow Pattern

Small Bow Pattern

Small Present Pattern Card Front

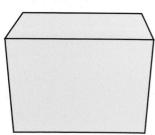

Flame Pattern   **Candle Pattern**

Cake Pattern Card Front

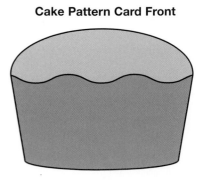

colorful candles

what you'll need

- Assorted card stock and textweight papers
- Oven-bake clay in assorted colors, such as Sculpey
- Rolling tool
- Pencil
- Crafts knife
- Scallop-edge scissors and pinking shears
- Glass baking dish and oven
- Paper punch; glue stick
- Thick white crafts glue
- Envelope or paper and tracing paper

greetings

May every candle burn brightly for you.

Make a wish!

here's how

1 Working on a smooth hard surface, roll out clay to approximately 1/8-inch thickness. Use a crafts knife or decorative-edge scissors to cut a candle shape from clay. Place candle shape on a glass baking dish.

2 To make clay dots, roll small amounts of clay between fingers and press onto candle shape, layering colors as desired. To make stripes, such as the green and yellow stripes, roll two lengths of colored clay several inches long and about 1/8-inch diameter. Pinch them together at one end. Hold the ends together and twist the colors from one end to the other. Cut and apply to candle.

3 To make flames, knead and roll orange and yellow clay together; roll into a small grape-size ball, press down flat, and shape a point. Press dots into the flame. Bake in oven on glass baking dish according to the clay manufacturer's instructions.

4 Choose card stock for card background. Measure and mark the fold line on the background card stock. Run a scoring tool, held with very little pressure, along the fold line. Fold the card stock in half along the score line.

5 To create an embossed look with stripes and dots, use a paper punch or cut strips of paper, layer paper on same color paper, and adhere using a glue stick. Use decorative scissors to cut paper shapes, layering from larger to smaller, and gluing with glue stick.

6 Use small amounts of crafts glue to adhere clay candles to card. Let dry.

7 To make an envelope, see *pages 109–110*. Cut coordinating paper strips with decorative scissors or punch paper dots and glue onto envelopes with a glue stick.

Shape funky birthday candles from oven-bake clay for a card that will be remembered even after the real candles have been blown out.

year-round holidays

Whether it's time for Easter egg hunts or decorating the Christmas tree, with each season comes a sense of family and friendship. And what better way to remember those you love than to make and send special cards you've created yourself. This festive chapter celebrates many occasions with inspiring ideas for integrating painting, clay, and paper cutting into your next holiday greetings.

ghostly greetings

Get in a ghoulish groove with this eerie-sistable card, brimming with ghosts and bats.

what you'll need

- 4-inch square of black card stock
- Two 8 ½×11 black card stock
- 2-inch circle of yellow-orange card stock
- 1 sheet white vellum; scrap of card stock
- Small scraps of moss green and tan card stock
- Tracing paper; pencil; scissors; spray adhesive
- Pigment ink in brown and white
- Brown puffy embossing powder; heat gun
- Glue stick; silver marking pen; batting
- Gel pens in white and colors; sewing thread in black and white
- Sewing needle; stippling brush
- Spray adhesive; glue stick
- Envelope or paper and tracing paper

here's how

1 Trace patterns, *opposite,* onto tracing paper. Cut a large ghost from vellum. Apply spray adhesive to back and adhere to front of black folded card.

2 Apply brown pigment ink directly to card stock in a circular fashion to create an inked area near the ghost. Apply embossing powder and heat.

3 From moss green card stock, cut out a tombstone, decorate as shown; glue to card above the embossed ink. Draw and cut out a hand from tan card stock; glue over grave.

4 With silver gel pen, draw in additional tombstones and the "BOO".

5 Glue a yellow-orange moon to card. Cut a small bat from black; glue to moon.

greetings

It's just me wishing you a Happy Halloween!

Have a spook-tacular trick-or-treat day!

6 Cut out a black spider. With white gel pen, draw spider legs, body, and eyes. Glue a 3-inch piece of white thread to back of spider. Pull apart batting, spray adhesive on back, and stick to card.

7 Lay thread over batting, over top of card and glue to the inside of front cover. With white pigment ink, stipple around ghost for a foggy look.

8 For inside of card, cut out small ghost and bat from card stock scraps. Layer shapes on inside card paper and stipple around edges with white pigment ink, reversing shapes.

9 With silver pen, write Happy Halloween and embellish with gel pen for outlines, eyes, pumpkins, and leaves.

10 Using black card stock scrap, cut out two bats. Outline both sides of each bat with white gel pen. Color eyes yellow with black center dot.

11 For each bat, thread a sewing needle with black thread, poke a hole in tip of bat wing, pull thread through and tie. Tie other end of thread to 12-inch length of black thread. Cut tiny slits in top right and left corners of inside card. Insert each end of black thread through the slit and glue to back of card. Adjust so when card is opened bats will "fly".

12 Glue inner card to outer card. Trim around edges. To make an envelope, see *pages 109–110*.

Large Bat Pattern

Tombstone Pattern

Large Ghost Pattern

Pumpkin Patterns

Small Ghost Pattern

Small Bat Pattern

Spider Pattern

rattling bones invite

Guests will know they're in for the party of a lifetime when they receive a hand-delivered clay skull and bones with their invitation.

what you'll need

- White air-dry clay, such as Crayola Model Magic; pencil; paper clip
- Medium-weight papers in purple, orange, and lime green
- Ruler; new quart-size paint can
- Thick white crafts glue; clear packing tape
- Envelope or paper and tracing paper

here's how

1 To make each bone, roll a finger-size piece of clay, center portion narrower than the ends. Pinch the ends slightly and make a notch in each end with a paper clip. Make six to eight bones for each invitation. Let the clay dry.

2 To make a skull, form a small clay pear shape. Larger end at the top, use a pencil point to make nasal cavities. Press a finger above nostrils to make eye sockets. To make the mouth, draw a wide U with a pencil. Press the end of a paper clip along the U to complete. Let dry.

3 Type an invitation on a 4×5-inch piece of lime green paper, leaving 1 inch at the top. Layer onto orange then purple papers, trimming as necessary to create narrow margins. Glue a bone to the top. Let dry.

4 Type a mailing label on orange paper; wrap around the can and tape the ends together. Trace lid on purple paper. Cut out ¼ inch within the line and glue to the lid. Let dry.

greetings

Get your bones over to our house...
(fill in invitation information)

∼∽

No bones about it, this party is going to rock!

∼∽

Pull yourself together and get over to our place for the scariest Halloween party ever!

∼∽

Mr. Missing Bones
3311 NW 81st Lane
Creepytown, USA

Miss Lindsay Johnson
707 East 7th Street
Hauntingtown, USA

GET YOUR BONES over to our house... (3311 NW 81st Lane) on OCTOBER 31st at 7:00 p.m.

No bones about it... it'll be the SPOOKIEST, silliest Halloween party EVER!

halloween hellos

Perfect for sending spirited salutations or invitations to a costume party, this boo-tiful pair of cards is just what the witch doctor ordered.

what you'll need

- Medium-weight paper in black, orange, white, and purple
- Plastic confetti star, bat, witch, jack-o'-lantern, ghost, moon, and circle shapes
- Ruler; pencil; scissors
- Toothpick
- Silver marking pen
- Glue stick
- Strong adhesive, such as E6000
- Envelope or paper and tracing paper

here's how

1 Cut black or orange background paper to measure 5×10 inches. Fold the paper in half, short ends together. The fold for these cards can be at the top or the left.
2 Cut a 4-inch square from black or orange. Use a glue stick to adhere the black square on the orange (window design) card and the orange square on the black (diamond design) card.
3 For window card, cut four 1¹/₂-inch white squares and glue to card in a window fashion as shown. For the diamond-design card, cut four 1¹/₂-inch squares from purple and glue to card in a diamond pattern as shown.
4 Use a toothpick to apply a dot of strong adhesive to the back of each confetti piece before placing on card. For stars, cut some in half to butt up to the edges of the borders. Glue confetti to cards as shown in the photograph, *above*. Let the glue dry.
5 Use a silver marking pen to draw ruled borders on each card.
6 To make an envelope, see *pages 109–110*.

greetings

The happiest of Halloweens to you and your ghoulish clan!

Spirited greetings to you!

Use a quick
stippling
technique to
create the
look of
fallen leaves
on this
Thanksgiving
beauty.

autumn shadows

what you'll need

- 1 sheet mustard brown card stock
- $1/2$ sheet white card stock
- $1/2$ sheet black card stock
- Various size/shape leaves from your yard
- Small die-cut oak leaf
- 4-5 colors of dye-based inks, such as Adirondak
- Crafts knife or scoring tool
- Stipple brush
- Gold gel pen
- Scissors; glue stick
- Envelope or paper and tracing paper

here's how

1 Cut mustard card stock to $5^1/_2\times11$ inches. Measure and mark the fold line on the card stock. Run a scoring tool, held with very little pressure, along the fold line. Fold the card stock in half along the score line.

2 Cut a 5-inch square of black card stock. Cut a $4^5/_8$-inch square of white card stock.

3 Using white card, lay one leaf at a time on the card, holding in place. With stipple brush, stipple one color around leaf. Remove and place another leaf on the card and stipple another color around it. Alternate leaves and paint colors for the desired effect. Let the paint dry.

4 Use gel pen to lightly draw veins on leaves.

5 Glue a die-cut oak leaf on the lower left-hand corner of the card front.

6 To make an envelope, see *pages 109–110*.

greetings

When I think of all I am thankful for, you are at the top of my list. Happy Thanksgiving!

Happy Autumn, Happy Thanksgiving!

Have a happy Thanksgiving, filled with all your favorite things!

thanksgiving blessings

what you'll need

- 10×7 patterned metallic gold card stock
- 5×7 patterned green card stock
- Pressed leaves or flowers
- Ruler
- Scoring tool
- Crafts knife
- Metallic gold marking pen
- Glue stick
- Envelope or paper and tracing paper

here's how

1 Measure and mark the fold line on the gold card stock. Run a scoring tool, held with very little pressure, along the fold line. Fold the card stock in half along the score line.

2 Measure and mark a window on the card front, leaving a $3/4$-inch frame all around. On a protected work surface, cut out the window using a crafts knife.

3 Use gold marking pen to write a message below the cutout. Outline the cutout window with gold. Let dry.

4 Arrange and adhere the pressed leaves in place on the green card stock using a glue stick. Glue the leafed piece to the back of the card-front frame.

5 To make an envelope, see *pages 109–110*. If desired, trim the envelope with a gold marker and glue a leaf on the flap.

greetings

I give thanks...for you.

You have given me the wonderful gift of your friendship. Thankful me.

Happy giving-thanks day from me to you!

oak leaf wishes

Let someone know they are in your thoughts with a lovely Thanksgiving greeting.

greetings

May your day be filled with all the beauty of nature, friendship, and family.

Here's hoping your Thanksgiving is one for the memory book.

what you'll need

- 4 coordinating metallic papers (1 textured)
- Dried, pressed leaf
- Scoring tool
- Ruler
- Pencil
- Gold spray paint
- Gold ribbon
- Spray adhesive
- White glue
- Glue stick
- Envelope or paper and tracing paper

here's how

1 Cut a $5^{1}/_{2} \times 10^{1}/_{2}$ rectangle of textured paper. Measure and mark the fold line. Score fold line, using a scoring tool held with very little pressure, along fold line. Fold paper in half. On the card front, trim $^{1}/_{2}$ inch from the two lower edges.

2 From contrasting papers, cut a $2^{1}/_{2}$-inch and a $2^{1}/_{4}$-inch square for the card front and a $5^{1}/_{2}$-inch square for the inside.

3 In a well-ventilated work area, cover work surface with newspapers. Spray leaf with gold spray paint. Let dry. Spray again if needed. Let dry.

4 Spray adhesive on the back of the large paper square and adhere it to the inside of the textured panel. Glue the remaining squares in the upper left corner, smaller square positioned on the larger square.

5 Tie ribbon onto leaf stem. Glue down leaf with small dabs of white glue.

6 To make an envelope, see *pages 109–110*. To embellish the flap, cut two diamonds in graduated sizes. Glue one tip in the center of the envelope flap.

seeded wreath

what you'll need

- 3 coordinating papers; coordinating card stock
- Colored peppercorns; mustard seed; raffia
- Pencil; pinking shears
- Bottle cap, small cup, or jar lid for pattern
- Paintbrush; glue stick; thick white crafts glue
- Envelope or paper and tracing paper

here's how

1 Trim base card stock to measure 9×5³/₄ inches. Measure and mark the fold line. Score fold line, using a scoring tool held with very little pressure, along fold line. Fold paper in half.

2 Trim a patterned paper panel 4¹/₂×5³/₄ inches. Glue on card front using a glue stick.

Cut a 2¹/₄-inch-wide strip from solid paper. Glue strip vertically on the center of the card.

3 Use pinking shears to cut narrow strips from contrasting paper. Glue strips to cover the edges of the solid paper.

4 Use pinking shears to trim the edges of the card front.

5 Using two round objects, such as a bottle cap and a jar lid, draw circles in pencil on the card front. Coat the circular band with glue, as shown in Photo A, *below left*.

6 Arrange peppercorns on glue then sprinkle the remainder of the glue with mustard seeds, as shown in Photo B. Let dry.

7 Glue a small raffia bow on the wreath. Let the glue dry.

8 To make an envelope, see *pages 109–110*.

The familiar wreath is welcome at Christmas or any time of the year. Made with peppercorns and mustard seeds, this ring is full of color.

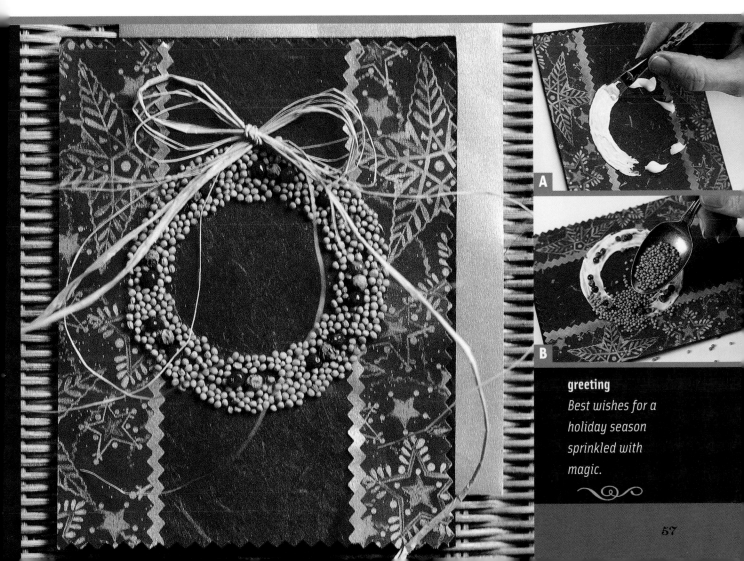

greeting
Best wishes for a holiday season sprinkled with magic.

christmas cutout card

Color a purchased wood cutout and dust with glitter for a sparkling Christmas wish.

greeting
Enjoy the season!

what you'll need

- $6^3/_4 \times 9^3/_4$ red card stock
- $6 \times 4^1/_4$ dotted vellum
- Snowflake photo corners
- Wood laser Christmas cutout
- Permanent marking pens
- Scoring tool
- Thick white crafts glue
- Envelope or paper and tracing paper

here's how

1 Measure and mark the fold line on the red card stock. Run a scoring tool, held with very little pressure, along the fold line. Fold the card stock in half along the score line. Place the vellum in the center of the card front and secure with photo corners.

2 Color the wood cutout as desired. To add interest to the cutout lettering, *below,* the top half was colored red and the bottom was colored dark pink.

3 Brush cutout with glue wherever glitter is desired. Sprinkle colored glitter on the glue. Let it dry.

4 Glue the cutout to the card front. Add dots of glue to the vellum and sprinkle with glitter to resemble snow. Let the glue dry.

5 To make an envelope, see *pages 109–110.* To trim envelope, glue glitter along the edge of the flap. Let the glue dry.

58

let it snow

greetings

Enjoy these snow-laden, bundle-up, chilled-nose kind of days!

I love these cuddle-up-with-me kind of days!

what you'll need

- $8^1/_2 \times 5^1/_2$ speckled white card stock
- $5^1/_2 \times 4^1/_4$ brown leather card stock; scrap of black card stock
- 10-inch length of $^1/_4$-inch-wide ribbon
- 8- and 10-inch lengths of gold craft wire
- 6-inch length of gold metallic thread
- 8-inch length of red-and-gold wired ribbon
- Black calligraphy pen, such as Zig Writer
- Scissors; corner punch
- Tiny hole punch; cellophane tape; glue stick
- Envelope or paper and tracing paper

here's how

1 Measure and mark fold line on speckled white card stock. Run a scoring tool, held with little pressure, along the fold line. Fold the card stock in half along the score line.

2 Cut a 1-inch strip from the brown leather card, dividing it into two sections. Punch the corners with a decorative punch. With calligraphy pen, write LET IT SNOW! on the narrow strip. Adhere both pieces to the white card, leaving a narrow space between.

3 Shape each wire into circles, $1^1/_2$- and $1^1/_8$-inch diameters. Open ends of circles together, knot the ribbon around both rings.

4 To cut the hat from the scrap of black card stock, fold a scrap in half. Beginning at the fold, cut the right rim, top of hat, then left rim. Trim away a slight part of the fold leaving a $^1/_8$-inch section in the center. Open flat, lay wire on the fold, apply glue to the top of the hat, then pinch closed. Punch a tiny hole in the hat top. Attach the metallic thread and knot the ends together.

5 Tie red ribbon into a small bow. Glue to top center of white card. Center ornament on brown card and pull metallic thread behind bow and over the top of the card. Attach to inside of card with tape.

6 To make an envelope, see *pages 109–110.*

nostalgic notes

what you need for the postcard greeting

- 5×12 red card stock
- Vintage or reproduction Christmas postcard
- Black photo corners
- Two metallic gold pipe cleaners
- Antique-edge scissors
- Envelope or paper and tracing paper

Send merry wishes by gracing a card with a vintage pin or postcard.

greetings

May the holidays calm your spirit and fill you with a sense of joy.

Wishing you an old-fashioned holiday.

here's how

1 Trim the red paper edges with antique-edge scissors. Fold the paper in half.

2 Use photo corners to adhere a postcard in the center of the card.

3 Wrap a pipe cleaner around the card fold. Twist the ends together to secure. Bend the remaining pipe cleaner in half. Twist the ends of the pipe cleaner on the card around the fold of the second pipe cleaner.

4 Wrap each pipe cleaner end around a pencil. Flatten the coils as desired. To make an envelope, see *pages 109–110*.

what you need for the pin card

- $5^3/_4 \times 11^1/_4$ white paper
- $5^1/_2 \times 11$ green print paper
- $4^1/_8$- and $1^7/_8$-inch squares crinkled metallic gold paper
- 3-inch square red and white polka-dot paper; scrap of dark green paper
- Vintage or reproduction Christmas pin
- 12 inches of $1/_2$-inch-wide sheer green ribbon
- Decorative-edge scissors; glue stick
- Thick white crafts glue
- Envelope or paper and tracing paper

here's how

1 Fold the white and green papers in half. Align the folds; glue green paper on top of the white paper.

2 Attach pin to the center of a dark green paper circle. Trim the paper with decorative-edge scissors.

3 Layer and glue the green paper to the center of the small gold paper. Glue the layers to the next larger piece.

4 Tie a ribbon bow. Use crafts glue to adhere the bow to the upper left side of the pin. Let the glue dry. To make an envelope, see *pages 109–110*.

the star in the east

This star is symbolic of the one that shone so bright over the manger. Sparkling beads in a row fall beautifully from the star.

what you'll need

- 8×8½ green card stock
- 8×8½ blue velour paper
- Green shank of seed beads
- Small thin wood star
- Green glitter
- Paper trimmer
- Scissors or crafts knife
- Glue stick; thick white crafts glue
- Envelope or paper and tracing paper

here's how

1 Fold the green paper in half, long edges together.

2 Use scissors to cut a freehand curve along one long edge of blue velour. Use a glue stick to adhere the back of the green panel to the inside of the blue panel.

3 Coat a small wood star with glue. Sprinkle green glitter on the wet glue, as shown in Photo A, shaking off excess glitter. Glue a strand of beads around the edge of the wood star. Let dry, and glue it on the blue panel. Let dry.

4 Draw glue lines extending from the star to the opposite edge of the card. Pull a strand from the shank of beads, without losing beads, and lay them on the glue, as shown in Photo B. Trim off the excess thread at the ends of the beads. Let dry.

5 To make an envelope, see *pages 109–110*. Draw a star and lines on the envelope flap and sprinkle with glitter. Let dry, and shake off excess glitter.

greeting
Blessings to you as we celebrate the birth of Jesus.

merry greeting

Send words of holiday cheer, even when time is running short. This last-minute card, donning sticker sentiments, will convey special wishes.

greeting
May all the goodness of this merry season be yours.

what you'll need

- 5¹/₂×9 light blue card stock
- Various-size sticker lettering, stars, and dots in silver and white; scoring tool
- Decorative-edge scissors
- Envelope or paper and tracing paper

here's how

1 Measure and mark fold line on card stock. Run a scoring tool, held with little pressure, along fold line. Fold card in half.

2 Plan placement of holiday words and phrases. Starting with the largest letters, peel and press into place. Fill in open areas with stars and dots.

3 To make an envelope, see *pages 109–110*.

4 **For the tag,** cut a piece of vellum in desired size. Back vellum with colored paper; trim beyond vellum using decorative-edge scissors. Press on sticker lettering. Punch a hole in one corner; thread ribbon through hole.

winter wonderland

Sequins sparkle like new-fallen snow on this merry holiday card. Use tube-style paint to write a sentiment all your own.

what you'll need

- Blue card stock
- White sequins
- White tube-style fabric paint
- Scoring tool; paper trimmer
- Pencil; circle template
- Scissors
- Thick white crafts glue
- Envelope or paper and tracing paper

here's how

1 Trim card stock to desired size. Measure and mark the fold line on the card stock. Run a scoring tool, held with very little pressure, along the fold line. Fold the card stock in half along the score line.

2 Use a pencil and circle template to mark corners; round corners with scissors.

3 Cover the bottom portion of the card with crafts glue and sprinkle on sequins. Dot the sky area with glue to randomly apply sequins.

4 Write a message on the card front using tube-style white paint. Let dry.

5 To make an envelope, see *pages 109–110*. Glue on sequins where desired.

greetings

Let your days sparkle with everything merry and bright!

Build a snowman. Make snow angels. Have a snowball fight. Enjoy the winter!

string snowman

With a head wound of string instead of snow, this friendly fellow will deliver jolly greetings all winter long.

Top Hat Pattern

Nose Pattern

what you'll need

- 6×12 textured red card stock
- 4$\frac{1}{2}$-inch square of light blue paper
- Black oven-bake clay, such as Sculpey
- Felt in orange and black
- Narrow red velvet ribbon; 1-inch-wide red and green plaid ribbon
- Natural string
- Glass baking dish and oven
- Thick white crafts glue
- Envelope or paper and tracing paper

here's how

1 Make seven half-pea-size balls from clay. Flatten slightly; place on baking dish. Bake in oven according to the manufacturer's instructions. Remove from oven; let cool.

2 Measure and mark the fold line on the card stock. Run a scoring tool, held with very little pressure, along the fold line. Fold the card stock in half along the score line. Center and glue the blue paper on the card.

3 Draw a 2$\frac{1}{2}$-inch diameter circle in the center of the blue paper. Fill in with glue.

4 Starting in the center of the circle, wind string to fill the circle. Let the glue dry.

5 Trace the hat and nose patterns, *right,* on tracing paper; cut out. Cut a hat from black felt and a nose from orange felt.

6 Arrange and glue the clay and felt pieces in place. Cut a piece from red velvet ribbon for hatband. Glue in place.

7 Tie a bow from plaid ribbon. Trim ends. Glue to the left of the snowman chin. Let dry.

8 Using a silver marking pen, highlight each of the clay pieces.

9 To make an envelope, see *pages 109–110.* Glue string loops on the flap.

greetings

May the season make you smile. Happy holidays!

Have a happy smile-on-your-face kind of day!

Send glad
tidings with
merry cards
that take just
minutes to
make.

what you'll need for the beaded candy cane card

- 5×10 green card stock
- 4-inch square white paper
- 2½-inch square red paper
- 1⅞-inch square green paper
- 2-inch-high beaded candy cane appliqué
- Glue stick; thick white crafts glue
- Envelope or paper and tracing paper

here's how

1 Measure and mark the fold line on the card stock. Run a scoring tool, held with little pressure, along the fold line. Fold the card stock in half along the score line.

2 Glue the white paper square in the center of the card front. Glue the red paper square in the center of the white square. Glue the green paper square on-point in the center of the red paper.

3 Glue the appliqué in the center of the green square using crafts glue.

4 To make an envelope, see *pages 109–110*. To trim flap, glue on coordinating paper strips.

what you'll need for the glittered stocking card

- 4½×8 red and white striped paper; 1½×1½ red paper
- 1¼×2¼ green paper
- 1⅞-inch-high glittered Christmas stocking sticker
- Glue stick
- Envelope or paper and tracing paper

here's how

1 Fold the red and white striped paper in half, short ends together.
2 Center and glue the red paper on the card front. Center and glue the green paper on the red.
3 Press the sticker in the center of the green paper.
4 To make an envelope, see *pages 109–110*.

what you'll need for the snowman appliqué card

- $4^1/_4 \times 9^1/_2$ **green card stock**
- $3^1/_2 \times 4$ **and** $2^3/_4 \times 3^1/_4$ **red paper**
- $3^1/_4 \times 3^3/_4$ **white paper**
- $2^3/_4$**-inch-high stitched snowman appliqué**
- **Glue stick; thick white crafts glue**
- **Envelope or paper and tracing paper**

here's how

1 Measure and mark the fold line on the card stock. Run a scoring tool, held with little pressure, along the fold line. Fold the card stock in half along the score line.
2 Center and glue the red and white papers on the card front.
3 Adhere the appliqué to the center of the card using crafts glue.
4 To make an envelope, see *pages 109–110*.

greetings

Wishing you all the joys of the season.

May your holidays sparkle with merriment.

Sending jolly wishes your way!

snowflakes and friends

what you'll need for the snowman card

- 4^1/$_2$×3^5/$_8$ black card stock
- 8^1/$_2$×5^1/$_8$ black card stock
- 4×4^7/$_8$ silver shimmer card stock
- Embossing paste
- Multi-colored ultra-fine glitter
- Silver pigment ink refill
- Snowman stencil
- Waxed paper; palette knife
- Double-face tape
- Old toothbrush and rubbing alcohol, optional
- Picture corner punch snowflake
- ^{1}/$_2$-inch removable tape
- Envelope or paper and tracing paper

here's how

1 On a hard flat surface use removable tape to secure stencil edges on small piece of black card stock; start with the bottom, then the top, and finally the sides.

2 On waxed paper place a small amount of embossing paste. (Use enough to stencil one time or as much as you are going to use for the project. The mixed paste will keep in a small airtight jar for about two weeks.) Mix with two or three drops of silver ink and some glitter.

3 Working quickly, pick up the paste on a palette knife. Smooth over the stencil area in one motion. Scrape off the excess until all the holes are filled evenly and the stencil surface is smooth. Take off the tape, leaving the bottom piece in place to use as a hinge. Lift the top of the stencil against the hinge; remove the hinge. Immediately clean stencil and palette knife in a shallow pan of water, scrubbing with an old toothbrush. If stencil has residue on it, clean with rubbing alcohol. Let dry for 30 to 60 minutes.

4 Score and fold remaining piece of black card stock in half. Punch corners of silver shimmer card stock. Insert corners of black card into slot on silver shimmer (you may have to trim black card to fit in slots on silver shimmer card). Use double face tape to assemble card.

5 To make an envelope, see *pages 109–110*.

what you'll need for the multiple snowflake card

- 8^1/$_2$×5^3/$_8$ black card stock
- 5^1/$_8$×4^1/$_8$ silver shimmer card stock
- 4×5 black mat board
- Snowflake and Merry Christmas stencils
- ^{1}/$_2$-inch removable tape
- Double-face tape
- Palette knife
- Ultra-fine multi-color glitter

- Silver pigment ink refill
- Embossing ink
- Embossing enamel
- Heat gun

here's how

1 On a hard flat surface, use removable tape to secure snowflake stencil edges to the black mat board, starting at the bottom, then the top, and finish with sides.

2 Mix paste and spread as for the snowman card, *left*. Repeat with the Merry Christmas stencil on the same black mat board. When paste is dry, apply embossing ink to the entire mat board, going over everything. Sprinkle embossing enamel on the mat board. Tap off excess, heat with heat gun. Repeat 2 or 3 times for a smooth finish.

3 Score and fold black card stock in half. Glue mat board to silver shimmer, then glue to card.

4 If you wish to make an envelope, see *pages 109–110*.

what you'll need for the single snowflake card

- 8^1/$_2$×5^1/$_4$ black and white card stock
- 3^1/$_4$-inch square of silver shimmer card stock
- 3-inch square of black mat board
- Merry Christmas and snowflake stencils
- Multi-color ultra-fine glitter
- Silver pigment ink refill
- Embossing ink
- Embossing enamel
- Heat gun
- ^{1}/$_2$-inch removable tape
- Double-face tape
- Palette knife

here's how

1 On a 3-inch-square black mat board, paste and heat emboss the snowflake stencil as in the instructions, *left*.

2 Score and fold black/white card stock in half, short ends together. Mount the embossed mat board on silver shimmer card. Adhere to the card front. Paste and heat emboss the Merry Christmas stencil on the lower portion of the card.

3 To make an envelope, see *pages 109–110*.

greetings

Fa-la-la-la-la!

~~~

Here's hoping that Santa is good to you!

~~~

Merry Christmas to our very best friends!

ornament card

Dress up circles to resemble tree trims. Topped with ornament caps and wire hangers, these tree-trimming tributes are close to the real thing.

what you'll need for the wonderland waves ornament cards

- 1 sheet of metallic card stock, choice of color
- 1 sheet of metallic silver card stock
- Metallic silver paper
- Glitter, 1-2 colors
- 6-inch piece of wire
- Circle cutter and mat
- Wire cutter
- Scissors
- Nail polish remover and soft cloth, optional
- Glue stick
- Peel-and-stick double-sided tape (must have the peeling)
- Envelope or vellum and tracing paper

here's how

1 Cut a 4-inch circle from metallic card stock.

2 Trace the patterns, *opposite,* on tracing paper; cut out. Trace around ornament cap twice on silver paper; cut out.

3 Cut a 5×2-inch rectangle from silver card stock. Cover the back of the rectangle with double-sided tape, then cut three curvy lines.

4 Wrap wire around something round, such as a large marking pen, at least twice to form the hanger; cut wire piece to include a complete circle.

5 Tape one ornament cap to front of ornament, as shown in photo, *opposite*. With ornament face down, put glue on ornament cap and attach wire ring. Align and glue second cap with front cap.

6 For ornament with curves, peel off paper and apply them to the front of ornament, leaving spaces in between to let the metallic background show through. Trim the outer edges of the wavy strips even with the round ornament.

7 Fill in spaces with glue; sprinkle glitter on the glue, shaking off any excess. Let dry. If you get glue or adhesive on the ornament, wipe it clean with nail polish remover and a soft cloth.

8 To make an envelope, see *pages 109–110*.

what you'll need for the snowy night card

- 1 sheet of blue metallic card stock
- 1 sheet of green metallic card stock
- Metallic silver paper
- 1 sheet vellum
- Metallic marking pens in silver and copper, such as Krylon or Painty Pen
- 6-inch length of wire
- Circle cutter and mat
- Scissors
- Wire cutter
- Nail polish remover and soft cloth, optional
- Spray adhesive
- Glue stick
- Envelope or vellum and tracing paper

here's how

1 Cut a 4-inch circle from blue metallic card stock.

2 Trace the patterns, *opposite,* on tracing paper; cut out. Trace around snow patterns on vellum; cut out two rolling snowy hills. Apply to blue circle with spray adhesive, overlapping as shown.

3 Cut out elongated triangles from green metallic card stock; glue to ornament as shown. With a silver pen, dot snowflakes and star. With copper pen, make tree trunks.

4 Using ornament cap pattern, cut two ornament caps from silver paper.

5 Wrap wire around something round, such as a large marker, at least twice to form the hanger; cut wire piece to include a complete circle.

6 Tape one ornament cap to front of ornament as shown in photo. With ornament face down, put glue on ornament cap and attach the wire ring. Align and glue the second cap with the front cap. If you get glue or adhesive on the ornament, wipe it clean with nail polish remover and a soft cloth.

7 To make an envelope, see *pages 109–110*.

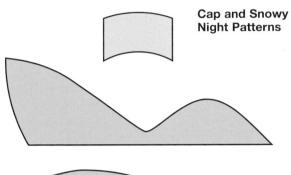

Cap and Snowy Night Patterns

jolly snowman card

With a wide grin beaming across a flat glass marble, this well-dressed snowman will make anyone's season merry and bright.

what you'll need

- 6×12 white card stock
- Patterned scrapbook papers in blue, green, and pink
- Tracing paper
- Flat clear or white marble
- Five small colored buttons
- Glass paint in black and orange
- Fine paintbrush
- Pencil
- Scissors; scoring tool
- Decorative-edge scissors
- Glue stick; thick white crafts glue
- Envelope or paper

here's how

1 Trace the patterns, *opposite*, onto tracing paper and cut out. Trace around the tree pattern on green scrapbook paper. Trace around the clothing pieces on pink, using one paper for the hat brim, coat, and corner triangles, and one pink paper for the hat and scarf. Cut out all shapes.

2 Paint a tiny carrotlike orange nose in the center of the marble. To make the snowman eyes and mouth, dip the handle of the paintbrush into black paint and dot above and below the nose. Let the paint dry.

3 Measure and mark the fold line. Score fold line, using a scoring tool held with very little pressure, along fold line. Fold paper in

half. Cut a 5-inch square from blue scrapbook paper. Use a glue stick to adhere it on the center of the card. Glue the tree and corner triangles in place.

4 Glue the coat and scarf in place. Using the marble to guide placement, glue the hat and brim in place.

5 Use thick white crafts glue to adhere the marble and buttons in place. Let dry.

6 To make an envelope, see *pages 109–110*. If desired, line the envelope flap with one of the scrapbook papers, gluing the right side of the paper to the underside of the envelope flap. Trim close to the envelope using decorative-edge scissors.

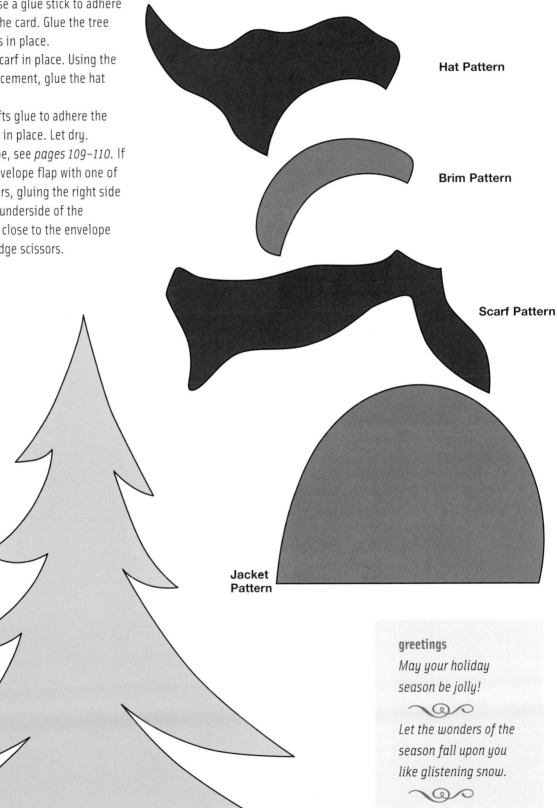

Hat Pattern

Brim Pattern

Scarf Pattern

Jacket Pattern

Tree Pattern

greetings
May your holiday season be jolly!

Let the wonders of the season fall upon you like glistening snow.

what you'll need for the tree card

- 10×7 red and white card stock
- 6¼×4¼ wine suede paper
- 6½×4½ gold shimmer paper
- Waxed paper
- Christmas tree and Merry Christmas stencils
- Translucent embossing paste
- Gold pigment ink refill
- Ultra fine gold glitter
- Palette knife
- Old toothbrush and rubbing alcohol, optional
- Pencil
- Ruler
- Scoring tool
- ½-inch removable tape
- Double-face tape
- Envelope or paper and tracing paper

here's how

1 On a hard flat surface, use removable tape to tape the tree stencil edges on the suede paper; start with the bottom, then the top, then the sides.

2 On a piece of waxed paper, place a small amount of embossing paste (enough to stencil one time or as much as you are going to use for the project; the mixed paste can be kept in a small airtight jar for about two weeks). Mix well with two or three drops of gold ink refill and some glitter.

3 Working quickly, pick up the paste on a palette knife, as you would load a knife for icing a cake. Smooth over the stencil area in one motion. Scrape off the excess until all the holes are filled evenly and the stencil surface is smooth.

4 Take off the tape, leaving the bottom piece in place to use as a hinge. Lift the top of the stencil against the hinge; remove the hinge. Immediately clean stencil and palette knife in a shallow pan of water and scrub with an old toothbrush. If stencil has residue on it, clean with rubbing alcohol. Let dry 30 to 60 minutes.

5 Repeat embossing with Merry Christmas stencil. Let dry.

6 Measure and mark the fold line on the background card stock. Run a scoring tool, held with very little pressure, along the fold line. Fold the card stock in half along the score line.

7 Mount suede paper to the gold then mount to card, using double-face tape to assemble. To make an envelope, see *pages 109–110*.

what you'll need for the bell card

- 11×4¼ green card stock
- ⅞-inch square red card stock
- 2¾-inch square holly print paper
- 2⅜-inch square gold shimmer paper
- 2¾-inch square wine suede paper
- Charm bell
- Merry Christmas stamp
- Pigment ink pad in gold
- Antique gold embossing powder
- Heat gun
- Envelope or paper and tracing paper

here's how

1 To make a tri-fold card, measure and score paper 3 inches from the left; fold to the back. Make a score mark 5 inches from the right and fold into a tri-fold card.

2 Layer and mount the holly print to the red card stock, adding the gold shimmer paper and wine suede. Mount the layers to front of the card as shown in the photo, *opposite*.

3 Affix charm bell to center of the suede. Stamp and heat emboss Merry Christmas inside.

4 To make an envelope, see *pages 109–110*.

greetings

Merry, Merry Christmas and a New Year to match!

Have a blessed holiday season.

Gilded embossed images are the central focus of these elegant holiday cards.

quilled valentine

what you'll need

- Card stock in light green, pink, and white
- White quilling paper strips
- Tracing paper
- Quilling tool
- Pencil
- Scissors
- Paintbrush
- White gel pen
- Glue stick
- Thick white crafts glue
- Envelope or paper and tracing paper

Send old-fashioned hugs and kisses with a beautifully quilled design.

here's how

1 Enlarge and trace the heart patterns, *below right*, onto tracing paper; cut out. Trace the largest heart onto pink, the next size on green. Trace the smallest heart onto pink paper and the larger heart onto white. Cut out the shapes. Layer the papers and glue together using a glue stick.

2 Using the quilling paper strips, make quilled circular or heart shapes. The shapes do not have to be perfectly equal or symmetrical, but can be random heart shapes and simple coils. To make a heart shape, first crease in the strand of paper near the center or off-center. This crease will become the bottom point of the heart shape. Coil each side of the heart inward or outward from the folded point. Insert one end of the quilling paper into the quilling tool and wind firmly (see Photo A, *below left*) up to the creased point, then gently release or unwind the coiled paper from the tool. Wind the other side in the same manner. Thinly coat one small area at a time with white glue, and place coiled heart shapes on the layered heart. Fill in bare spots with simple coils.

3 Write a message on the small layered hearts and glue in place on top of valentine.

4 To make an envelope, see *pages 109–110*. Glue a paper heart to the flap.

Valentine and Inset Heart Patterns

1 square = 1 inch
Reproduce at 400%

greeting
You are the love of my life!

watercolor wishes

greeting

Have I told you yet today that I love you?

what you'll need

- Watercolor paper; coordinating colored papers; watercolor paints
- Air-dry clay, such as Crayola Model Magic
- White pearl acrylic paint; ribbon
- White iridescent glitter; fine gold wire
- Tiny seed beads
- Medium round watercolor paintbrush
- Rolling pin; heart shape cookie cutter; salt
- Scissors; glue stick; thick white crafts glue

here's how

1 Thoroughly soak watercolor paper and lay it on a smooth, flat surface. Experiment with paint color by combining such colors as magenta, purple, orange-yellow, and lime green.

2 Begin to work with the paint when the water on the surface of the paper begins to soak in and before it dries. Fill the round paintbrush with concentrated paint color. Brush, dot, or dabble onto the wet paper, as shown in Photo A, *right.* The paint should bleed as the brush touches the paper. Before it dries, paint another color next to it to bleed together. Add colors, painting in swirls if desired, and work quickly while the paper remains wet.

3 When the paper is painted and the surface is visibly wet but not soaked, sprinkle lightly with salt where you want spotted texture, as shown in Photo B. The salt will soak up the color from the paper. Let dry.

4 Brush dried salt off painting. Cut the painted paper into rectangles for a card. Make a card by layering and gluing coordinating colored papers.

5 To make textured hearts, roll out clay to $^1/_8$-inch thickness. Cut out heart shapes with cookie cutter, as shown in Photo C. Let dry.

6 Paint hearts with white pearl acrylic paint. Before the paint dries, sprinkle with glitter.

7 String tiny, multicolored seed beads onto a length of wire to extend from the heart, avoiding stringing beads right behind the heart.

8 Lay down wired beads and glue the heart in place on top of the wire. Weigh it down with a heavy object until it dries, if necessary.

9 Add decorative ribbons loosely tied at the fold. Trim the ribbon ends. To make an envelope, see *pages 109–110.*

A

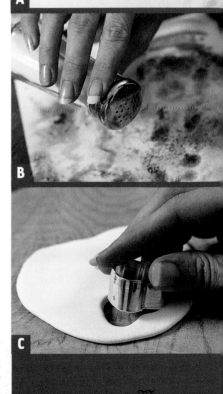

B

C

you-have-my-heart card

With three embossed stamps, two folds, and a frame, this fancy card design will steal hearts.

what you'll need

- Red card stock,
  11×5$\frac{1}{2}$ inches, 3$\frac{1}{4}$- and 3-inches square,
  and 2$\frac{1}{2}$×1$\frac{3}{4}$ inches
- Silver shimmer card stock in 5$\frac{1}{4}$-inches
  square, 3$\frac{1}{4}$-inches square, and 2$\frac{3}{4}$×2 inches
- Small rosebud heart rubber stamp
- Small rosebud rubber stamp
- With Loving Thoughts rubber stamp
- Silver pigment ink pad
- Silver embossing powder
- Ruler
- Pencil
- Scoring tool
- Crafts knife
- Heat gun
- Glue stick
- Envelope or paper and tracing paper

here's how

1 Laying the red 11×5$\frac{1}{2}$-inch card stock horizontally, measure, mark, and score the card stock 2$\frac{3}{4}$ inches from the left edge. Make a second score line 5$\frac{1}{2}$ inches from the right edge. Fold the flaps to the center.

2 Using the 5$\frac{1}{4}$-inch piece of silver shimmer card stock, cut out a 3$\frac{3}{4}$-inch square from the center to make a frame. Mount the frame to left flap only, as shown in the photo, *opposite*. Use the 3$\frac{3}{4}$-inch square that was cut from the frame and trim it to measure 3$\frac{1}{2}$ inches square; mount to the right flap only, so when the card is closed it is centered in the frame.

3 Stamp the rosebud heart design on the 3$\frac{1}{4}$-inch square of red card stock. Heat emboss the design in silver. Glue the embossed design to the center of the square on the right flap.

4 On the 3-inch square red card stock, stamp and heat emboss the phrase stamp in silver. Glue the embossed piece on the 3$\frac{1}{4}$-inch square silver shimmer card stock; mount to the inside center of the card.

5 Stamp and heat emboss the two 2$\frac{1}{2}$×1$\frac{3}{4}$-inch rectangles of red card stock with a small rosebud; glue one on each remaining piece of silver shimmer card stock. Glue the pieces on each inside cover.

6 To make an envelope, see *pages 109–110*.

greetings

With Loving Thoughts

You will be in my heart forever.

You've touched my heart and I wanted you to know.

Inside of Card

lacy valentine

what you'll need

- 14×7¹/₂ decorative pink card stock
- 7×7¹/₂ white card stock
- Rhinestones
- Ruler; scoring tool
- Tracing paper; pencil
- Scissors
- Crafts knife; kneaded eraser
- Glue marker pen; white glitter
- Glue stick
- Thick white crafts glue
- Envelope or paper and tracing paper

here's how

1 Measure and mark the fold line on the pink card stock. Run a scoring tool, held with very little pressure, along the fold line. Fold the card stock in half along the score line.

2 Fold tracing paper in half. Aligning folds, trace the heart pattern onto tracing paper and cut out. Place heart pattern on back of card, aligning top edge of heart with the fold of card. Draw heart outline ¹/₈ inch beyond pattern. Cut out heart shape, allowing two uncut portions at card top for hinge.

3 Trace around decorative heart on white card stock. On a protected work surface, cut out design using a crafts knife. Erase any pencil lines with a kneaded eraser.

4 Spread on glue with a glue marker. Quickly sprinkle on white glitter; shake off excess.

5 Use white glue to apply rhinestones.
6 To make an envelope, see *pages 109–110*. To embellish an envelope, draw a row of hearts on the flap and sprinkle with glitter. Glue on rhinestone accents.

Fold

Cutout Heart Pattern

easter blessings

what you'll need

- Gold card stock
- White card stock
- Colored mottled background paper
- Colored papers for flowers, such as mulberry papers
- Dimensional glitter paint
- Beads for flower centers and blue flowers
- Fine gold wire
- Paper trimmer with ruler
- Tracing paper
- Pencil
- Crafts knife
- Embossing marker
- Embossing powder
- Heat gun
- Raised glue tabs
- Tiny scissors
- Spray adhesive; white glue
- Toothpick
- Envelope or paper and tracing paper

here's how

1 Trim gold card stock to 10^1/$_2$×7^1/$_4$ inches. Measure and mark fold line at 5^1/$_4$ inches. Score fold line. Run a scoring tool along fold line. Fold paper.

2 Use a decorative mottled paper for the main panel. Cut the paper slightly smaller than the front panel and affix with glue stick to front.

3 Trace the cross patterns, *opposite,* onto tracing paper, cut out and trace onto white paper; cut out. Trace floral pieces onto colored papers; cut out.

4 For small flowers, use small pieces of lightweight mulberry paper adhered together for different effects. The leaves are green paper glued to blue. The pink flowers are pink on one side and orange on the other. Use a glue stick to adhere papers together. Set flowers aside.

5 Use an embossing marker, embossing powder, and heat gun to add gold embossing to crosses, leaves, and card edges. To emboss, mark one section with the pen, quickly sprinkle powder onto marked area before it dries, shake off excess, and heat with heating tool to emboss. Embossing can be reheated. When finished with crosses, affix adhesive raised tabs on the larger cross. Center small cross on the large cross.

Pretty enough to display every year, this detailed Easter card is embellished with cut-paper flowers and tiny beads.

greeting
Blessed Easter greetings.

6 Lay the assembled cross on the center of the card panel and trace around it lightly with a pencil.

7 Shape paper flowers, and glue them onto the card with a dab of white glue. For the daisies, cut circles from pink, cut fringes toward the center, and curl them up. Fold the lilies from the bottom sides over. Use a toothpick to apply glue. Insert a tiny wire with gold beads glued to the ends. Crease and shape the leaves to add dimension. Use tube-style glitter paint to apply a bead to daisy center and to glue the blue beads in place in the corners.

8 Use raised glue tabs to adhere cross to card.

9 To make an envelope, see *pages 109–110*.

Cross Pattern

1 square = 1 inch
Reproduce at 200%

Leaf Pattern

Leaf Pattern

Leaf Pattern

Flower Pattern

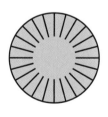

Lily Bud Pattern

Lily Pattern

happy easter eggs

Send Easter
greetings
with large
colorful
paper eggs
that bring
springtime
joy.

what you'll need

- 8×5³/₄ card stock for background
- Coordinating card stock papers in bright colors and white
- Scoring tool
- Tracing paper; pencil; scissors
- Pinking shears and/or decorative-edge scissors
- Paper punch for rivets; hammer
- Color marking pen
- Paper punches in stars and dots; glue stick
- Envelope or paper and tracing paper

here's how

1 Using the background card stock, measure and mark the fold line. Run a scoring tool, held with very little pressure, along the fold line. Leave card unfolded.

2 Enlarge and trace the desired egg pattern, *below,* onto tracing paper. (The cards at the size shown, *opposite,* use the purple pattern.) Cut out the egg shape. *To make purple egg card with rectangular back,* trace the egg shape on the front card panel only; cut out. *To make the folded egg shape,* fold the card stock in half along the score line, short ends together. Trace egg onto the card back aligning one edge on the fold; cut out shape through both layers of paper, leaving a portion of the fold.

3 Use pinking shears and decorative-edge scissors to cut strips, squares, or shapes, and use small paper punches to make additional shapes. Layer and arrange the papers as desired, smaller shapes on larger ones. Adhere in place using a glue stick.

4 Punch holes last, using a paper punch for making rivets. Place card on a hard protected surface, position punch, and pound with a small hammer.

5 Write a message with a marking pen.

6 To make an envelope, see *pages 109–110.* Embellish the flap with coordinating paper strips and dots.

greetings
Happy egg hunting!

Here's hoping the Easter bunny brings you a basket full of special surprises!

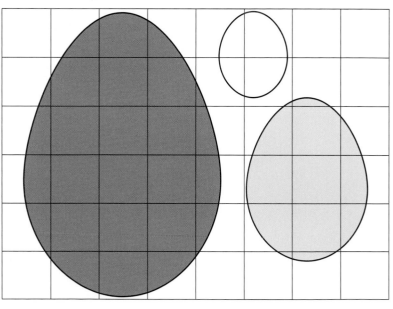

Egg Patterns

1 square = 1 inch
Enlarge at 200%

Happy Easter

patriotic duo

what you'll need for the heart card

- 8$\frac{1}{2}$×5$\frac{1}{2}$ white card stock
- 3$\frac{1}{4}$×4$\frac{1}{2}$ red card stock
- 3×4 blue polka-dot paper
- 3$\frac{1}{2}$×5 aluminum foil
- Pinking shears
- Heart-shape cookie cutter; crafts knife
- Star-shape paper punch
- Silver marking pen
- Glue stick
- Envelope or paper and tracing paper

here's how to make the heart card

1 Measure and mark the fold line on the white card stock. Lightly run a scoring tool along the fold line. Fold the card stock in half.

2 Trace around a heart cookie cutter in the center of the card front. With the card open on a hard flat work surface, cut out the shape using a crafts knife. Mark and cut three $\frac{1}{4}$-inch-wide stripes extending from the heart to the lower right-hand corner of the card as shown, *right.* Punch out star shapes around the left edge of heart. Draw small silver dots around the heart.

3 Trace heart shape in center of foil. Cut out slightly larger. Glue foil to back of red card stock. Trim foil just beyond red edges using pinking shears. Fold foil edge to front of card stock. Glue blue polka-dot paper behind heart. Glue layered piece to the front of card. To make an envelope, see *pages 109–110.*

what you'll need for the cutout card

- 9×5$\frac{1}{2}$ and 4$\frac{1}{2}$×5$\frac{1}{2}$ white card stock; crafts knife
- Patterned scrapbook papers in blue and red
- Silver marking pen; tape; glue stick
- Envelope or paper and tracing paper

here's how to make the cutout card

1 Measure and mark the fold line on the white card stock. Lightly run a scoring tool along the fold line. Fold the card stock in half.

2 Open card. Use a ruler and pencil to mark openings on the front, as shown, *right.* On a hard flat work surface, cut out windows using a crafts knife.

3 Cut scrapbook papers, slightly larger than each opening. Tape to window backs. Glue a larger paper on the back to secure the small patterned pieces.

4 Draw dashed lines around openings with a silver pen.

5 To make an envelope, see *pages 109–110.* Cut and glue scrapbook paper on the flap. Outline with dotted silver lines.

Show your pride for America by sending a meaningful message on a red, white, and blue note card. Patterned scrapbook papers add a homey touch to the creation.

greetings

Happy Independence Day! Show your colors!

Here's hoping your Fourth of July is filled with picnics, fun, and fireworks!

to my friend...

my dearest...

just because

Brighten someone's day just for the fun of it! This pretty card collection uses a variety of techniques— stamping, tearing, printing, embossing, and more— to make your cards extra special. Whoever is on your mind, there's a card waiting to let them know.

asian influence

greetings

*Thinking of you and
what a beautiful person
you are.*

*May our friendship be a
comfort during this
difficult time.*

what you'll need

- $8^{1}/_{2}\times5^{1}/_{4}$ white card stock
- $3^{1}/_{2}\times3$-inch square white card stock
- $3^{3}/_{4}\times3^{1}/_{4}$ gold shimmer paper
- $8^{1}/_{2}\times5^{1}/_{4}$ red and white fibrous silk paper
- $5\times3^{7}/_{8}$ Asian-print paper
- Butterfly with ferns rubber stamp
- Butterfly charm
- Ruler; pencil; scoring tool; gold pigment ink pad
- Clear embossing powder; heat tool
- Glue stick; thick white crafts glue
- Envelope or paper and tracing paper

here's how

1 Measure and mark a score line on large piece of white card stock. Lightly run a scoring tool along fold line. Fold paper. Glue red silk paper then Asian paper to card front.

2 Use rubber stamp to stamp gold designs on white card stock. Emboss with clear powder.

3 Glue the embossed paper in the center of the gold shimmer paper; adhere to card to the left of center.

4 Use crafts glue to adhere butterfly charm on the stamped butterfly. Let dry.

5 To make an envelope, see *pages 109–110.*

embossed medallion card

Natural fibers and torn textured papers cradle a cardboard shape that's draped in colored ink and embossing enamel.

what you'll need

- Pigment inks in red, black, and gold
- Cardboard shape
- Embossing enamel
- 8¹/₂×5¹/₂ mustard card stock
- Various scraps of mulberry and/or natural fiber papers of your choice
- 3-inch length of twine
- Rubber stamp in an Asian or other design
- Heat gun; scissors; thick white crafts glue
- Envelope or paper and tracing paper

here's how

1 Apply red ink to cardboard shape, covering it completely. Apply the embossing enamel; heat; then cool. Repeat twice.

2 With gold ink, press the pad onto the red enamel in one or two places. Apply embossing enamel to gold; heat. While heating, the gold will spread over the red. Continue until the desired effect is achieved. Let cool.

3 Apply black ink to the rubber stamp. Heat the embossed shape in the area for the stamped image until the colors begin to spread. Immediately apply the rubber stamp to the hot enamel, pressing hard. Leave the stamp until the enamel has had time to cool. Repeat in other areas as desired.

4 Score and fold card stock in half. Tear or cut mulberry papers or natural fiber papers. Arrange on card and glue in place. Glue the embossed shape to card. Tie knot in twine and glue to card. Let the glue dry.

5 To make an envelope, see *pages 109–110.*

greetings

Relax...unwind...and enjoy some peace and quiet. You deserve it!

You are in my thoughts, today and always.

glitterfly card

what you'll need

- $4^1/_2 \times 5^1/_2$ black card stock
- $10 \times 6^1/_4$ gold metallic parchment
- $1 \times ^1/_2$ scrap of card stock paper
- Two leaf rubber stamps; metallic gold ink pad
- Light blue ink pad; fine copper glitter
- Decorative punch
- Scissors; glue stick
- Envelope or $6^1/_2 \times 13$-inch piece of gold card stock or other paper and tracing paper

here's how

1 *For the butterfly,* use your little finger as a stamp to make five dots in a row in the middle of the black card stock, as shown in Photo A, *left.* Choose one of the leaf stamps and make the "wings" on either side of the fingerprints using gold ink. Repeat with the other leaf stamp for another set of wings using light blue ink. *For the flower,* use leaf stamp to make five or six petals on black card stock.

2 Lightly dust the ink with copper glitter.

3 For antennae, slightly bend the scrap of card stock and dip the edge in the ink. Print at the top of the body, as shown in Photo B. Set aside.

4 Score and fold the metallic parchment in half. Using the decorative punch, punch the bottom of the card. Glue the black cardstock on the gold parchment.

5 To make an envelope, see *pages 109–110,* or score and fold the gold cardstock 1 inch from an edge. Score and fold again 6 inches from that fold. Seal the side edges with glue. Glue a small triangle of black card stock to the flap.

6 **For the tag,** cut a paper background. Cut a slightly smaller piece from contrasting paper. Glue papers together. Stamp desired design on smaller piece. Punch a hole in one corner.

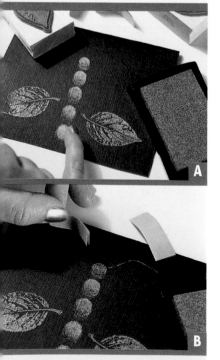

Leaf stamps and fingerprints create one-of-a-kind designs to add personality to note cards.

ribbons and flowers

A sheer ribbon stitched to the card front creates a backdrop for the pastel posies. Layers of dainty papers cut in flower shapes complete the lovely presentation.

what you'll need

- 8×9 heavyweight fibered papers in violet, yellow, or pink
- 8×9 pastel color light weight bond paper sheets
- Fibrous tissue papers in white, pink, green, and purple
- Wide ribbon
- White thread
- Clear rhinestones
- Sewing machine
- Thick white crafts glue; glue stick
- Adhesive, such as Beacon Gem-Tac glue
- Pastel color standard-size business envelopes

here's how

1 Before machine-stitching the card, sew on a heavyweight fibered and bond paper scrap on your sewing machine to test and adjust the tension. Repeat the process with ribbon and fibrous paper scrap.

2 Stack the heavyweight fibered paper over a matching pastel bond sheet and fold the short ends together. Unfold the card, two layers stacked together. Machine-stitch the two layers together along the length of the fold line.

3 Fold the inside bond paper to one side and stitch a length of ribbon along the center front of the card. Trim the ribbon and thread ends even with the paper edge. Prevent the stitching from unraveling by dabbing a dot of crafts glue at the end of each seam.

4 Cut pattern pieces from lightweight tissue paper, and use the glue stick to attach them along the ribbon. Use adhesive to glue a rhinestone in the center of each flower.

5 To make an envelope, see *pages 109–110*.

greetings

I hope this brightens your day as much as you brighten all of mine!

Thank goodness for you!

I miss you and can't wait until we're together again.

Flower and Leaf Patterns

daffodil days

You don't need a garden to give the gift of a daffodil. Emboss it on the front of a card for a delicate remembrance any time of the year.

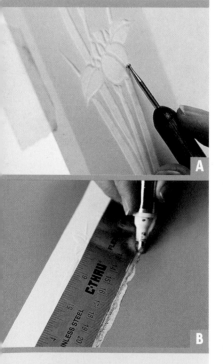

greetings

*Wishing I was there
... or you were here!*

~◦~

*Thinking of you
during this
difficult time.*

~◦~

what you'll need

- Ivory card stock; scoring tool
- Yellow textured paper
- Yellow and white check paper
- Daffodil embossing template
- Embossing tool
- Light box or window
- Gold marking pen
- Gold cord; glue stick
- Tape
- Envelope or paper and tracing paper

here's how

1 Tape embossing template onto light box (or window) and tape ivory card stock over it.

2 Use embossing tool to emboss ivory card stock template until image is completely visible, as shown in Photo A, *left*. Make sure to emboss into every corner and surface.

3 Remove embossed paper and trim to 3×5³/₄ inches. Tear off one edge; lay a ruler down to draw a gold marker line along edge, as shown in Photo B. Let dry.

4 Cut a 5³/₄×9-inch yellow textured card stock. Measure and mark a score line. Lightly run a scoring tool along fold line. Fold paper.

5 Glue a coordinating panel of paper onto front of card allowing ivory card stock to show along the right edge. Glue the embossed piece on card front.

6 Tie a gold cord along fold of card.

7 To make an envelope, see *pages 109–110*. Draw a wide gold rule along the edge of the envelope flap.

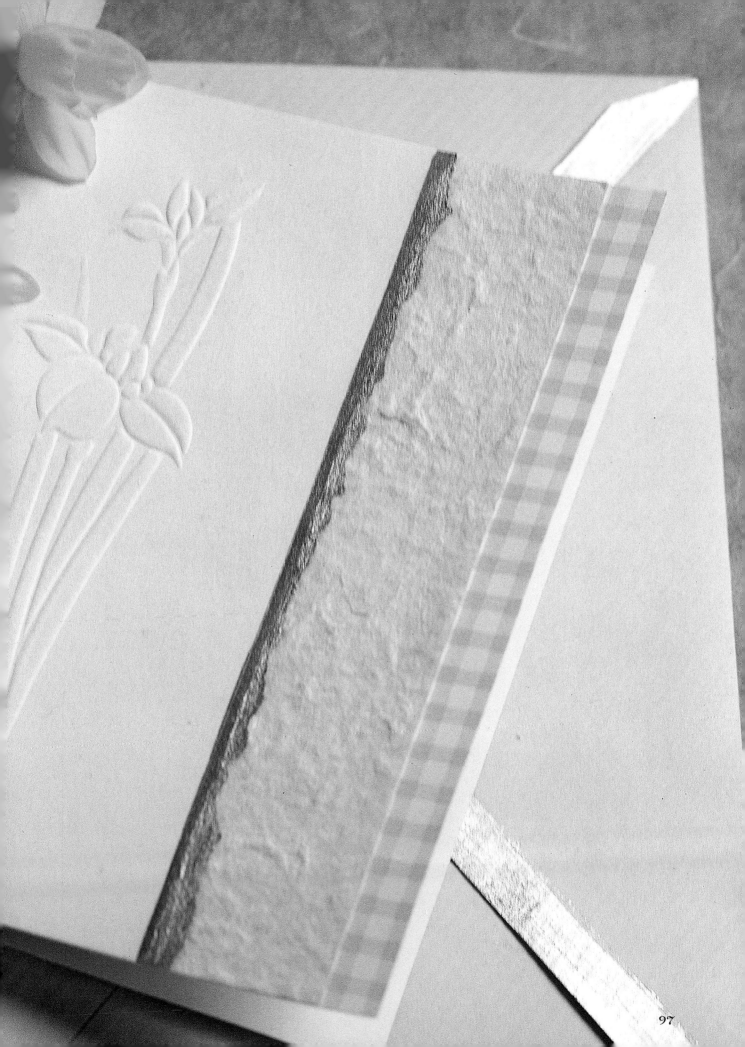

lasting impressions

Stamped
air-dry clay
adds special
touches to
these gilded
cards for
friends and
spouses.

what you'll need
- Card stock in white and gold
- White air-dry clay, such as Crayola Model Magic
- Clay stamp
- Gold stamp pad
- Paper trimmer
- Scoring tool
- Gold button
- Wire cutter
- Thick white crafts glue
- Glue stick
- Envelope or paper and tracing paper

here's how
1 Roll a small amount of white clay to approximately $1/8$-inch thickness. Use a stamp to press an image into the clay. To tear the edges, let the clay dry until it will tear without stretching.

2 Trim gold card stock to desired size to fit your envelope. Measure and mark the fold line on the card stock. Run a scoring tool, held with very little pressure, along the fold line. Fold the card stock in half along the score line.

3 If desired, layer and glue more torn papers to fit the card. Glue clay piece on card front using crafts glue.

4 To attach a button, clip off the back of button with wire cutters; glue in place with crafts glue. If desired, tie gold ribbon around the fold of the card.

5 To make an envelope, see *pages 109–110*. Use same stamp used on the clay to embellish the envelope. Stamp onto gold ink pad and apply to the envelope.

greetings

You make life worth living.

I am so blessed to have you in my life!

purple and copper

A dazzling combination— purple, gold, and copper— create an unforgettable message of love.

what you'll need

- 5×8 gold or copper card stock
- Tube-style fabric paint in copper and glitter gold
- Purple acrylic paint
- Purple gems
- Scoring tool
- Medium flat paintbrush
- Decorative-edge scissors
- Glue stick
- Envelope or paper and tracing paper

here's how

1 Measure and mark score line on card stock. Run a scoring tool, held with very little pressure, along fold line. Fold paper along the score line.

2 Generously paint a small piece of card stock using copper dimensional paint, leaving brush marks in the paint for interesting texture. Let dry.

3 Paint another scrap of paper purple. Let dry. Trim a rectangular piece from the purple and write your message in glitter paint. Draw swirls on the remainder of purple.

4 Trim the edges of the copper and purple papers with decorative-edge scissors. Using the photo, *below,* for inspiration, layer and glue the papers on the front of the card using a glue stick. Use crafts glue to adhere purple gems below the purple paper strip.

5 To make an envelope, see *pages 109–110.* Use fabric paint to apply gems on the envelope flap. Let dry.

charming note cards

Trimmed with decorative-edge scissors, these summer-hue papers create a soft background for gold metal charms.

what you'll need
- Card stock in yellow, pale green, medium green, periwinkle, and purple
- Metallic gold metal charms
- Straight-edge and decorative-edge scissors
- Thick white crafts glue; needle-nose pliers
- Envelope or paper and tracing paper

here's how
1 Cut a $9^1/_4 \times 5^1/_8$-inch yellow paper for the square card or a $6^5/_8 \times 5^1/_2$-inch pale green paper for the rectangular card. Measure and mark the fold line on the card stock. Run a scoring tool, held with little pressure, along the fold line. Fold the card along the score line.

2 For the square card, use decorative-edge scissors to cut medium green paper 8×4 inches. Fold in half with the short ends together. Glue over the yellow paper. Cut four $1^1/_4$-inch squares, two from yellow and two from pale green. Center and glue on front of card, leaving $^1/_8$-inch margin between squares.

3 For the rectangular card, use straight scissors to cut a $4^1/_2 \times 2^1/_2$-inch blue paper. Glue blue rectangle on purple paper. Trim purple paper close to blue paper using decorative-edge scissors. Glue in center of card front. Cut a $^7/_8 \times 3^1/_8$-inch piece from pale green. Glue in center of card front.

4 Remove hanging loops from charms if necessary, bending with pliers. Glue charms on card front. Let the glue dry.

5 To make an envelope, see *pages 109–110*.

To make an envelope, see *pages 109–110*.

greetings
Just thinking about you...and wanted you to know.

I'm sorry...so very sorry.

bracelet card

Tuck a bracelet for a little girl to wear in this beaded heart card. Choose a pretty button to top off the sentiment.

what you'll need

- 4×8 card stock
- 3½-inch square check paper
- Large seed beads
- Beading elastic
- Decorative button
- Crafts knife or scoring tool
- Corner rounder
- Pencil
- Needle and thread
- Red marking pen; glue stick
- Coordinating envelope

here's how

1 Make two bracelets using elastic and seed beads. String on a button and knot the elastic ends. Trim off excess elastic.

2 Measure and mark the fold line on the card stock. Lightly run a scoring tool, held with very little pressure, along the fold line. Fold the card stock in half along the score line.

3 Use a corner rounder on the corners of the check paper; adhere to the card front.

4 Lightly draw a heart shape on the center of the card with a pencil to use as a guide to sew on bracelet with a needle and thread.

5 Write message inside heart. To make an envelope, see *pages 109–110.*

6 **For the tag,** cut paper with decorative-edge scissors. Cut contrasting paper for the center. Punch a hole in one corner. Thread with beaded ribbon.

sunshiny sentiments

The striking foursome of sunglasses are plastic buttons with the shanks removed. With sunglasses mounted to vivid paper squares, this card is filled with sunshiny wishes.

what you'll need

- $4^{1}/_{4} \times 8^{1}/_{2}$ yellow card stock
- $3^{3}/_{4} \times 8$ iridescent white paper
- $^{1}/_{8}$-inch-wide orange satin ribbon
- Four plastic sunglass buttons
- Scraps of paper in the four colors of the glasses frames
- Paper punch
- Scissors; pliers; ruler; pencil
- Fine-line black marking pen
- Glue stick
- Envelope or paper and tracing paper

here's how

1 Fold the yellow paper in half, short ends together. Fold the white paper in half, short ends together. Place the white paper over the yellow paper, aligning folds. Use a paper punch to make two holes approximately $^{1}/_{2}$ inch from the folded edge.

2 Thread orange ribbon through the holes and tie a bow in the center. Trim the ribbon ends.

3 Use pliers to twist off the button shanks.

4 From each of the four colors of paper scraps, cut a $1^{1}/_{2} \times 1^{5}/_{8}$-inch piece to back sunglasses, adjusting this size to fit the buttons.

5 Use a glue stick to adhere the paper windowpane fashion on the card front. Glue each of the sunglasses at an angle on a paper rectangle using crafts glue. Let the glue dry.

6 Write WISHING YOU SUNSHINE! on the yellow strip along the lower border.

7 To make an envelope, see *pages 109–110*. To trim envelope, punch a row of holes on the flap.

greetings

Hope your day is as bright and lovely as you are!

You've got it made in the shade!

delicate dragonflies

what you'll need

- 4¹/₄×5¹/₂ card stock
- 8¹/₂×5¹/₂ card stock
- Dye-based ink pads in 3 to 5 colors
- Brush markers in 5 desired colors
- Dragonfly rubber stamp
- Stipple brush
- Smooth plastic lid, such as margarine tub lid
- Fine-mist spray bottle
- Pencil
- Ruler
- Crafts knife
- Cutting mat
- Scoring tool
- Removable tape, such as blue masking tape
- Envelope or paper and tracing paper

here's how

1 To make the stippling template, draw a 4-pane window on the 4¹/₄×5¹/₂ card stock, leaving ¹/₄-inch cross bars. Using a crafts knife, mat, and ruler, cut out the four squares.

2 Measure and mark the fold line on the 8¹/₂×5¹/₂-inch piece of card stock. Run a scoring tool, held with very little pressure, along the fold. Fold the card stock in half along the score line. Lay the template on the card front and tape it to a work surface.

3 With a stipple brush and dye ink pads, stipple each corner of the squares starting with the darkest color. Working dark to light, outside to inside, stipple each square. Place template on front of envelope in desired position and repeat stippling using only one square.

4 With the brush markers, color on the margarine lid in no particular pattern. Do not overlap colors but get them as close as possible. Use a water bottle to lightly spritz the ink. Press the dragonfly rubber stamp on the ink, then stamp on the card front and envelope. You may need to repeat coloring and spritzing the lid as you stamp. Wipe the lid clean with a paper towel and start over with brush markers.

5 To make an envelope, see *pages 109–110*.

A stippled window in soft tones makes an enchanting backdrop for dragonflies in flight.

greetings
Hoping your day is carefree and fun!

∽ᴏᴏᴐ∼

I miss you— let's get together soon for lunch!

∽ᴏᴏᴐ∼

a friendly reminder

Surprise your best friend with a greeting as special as your relationship. The interesting fold on this card accents the message of endearment.

greeting

It's time for a girls' night out—let's go!

what you'll need

- 2 coordinating papers, one patterned and one solid
- Coordinating solid card stock
- Paper trimmer
- Ruler
- Pencil
- Crafts knife
- Coordinating pencil or marker
- Spray adhesive
- Glue stick
- Envelope or paper and tracing paper

here's how

1 Spray the back side of patterned paper with adhesive and carefully align corners of the solid paper, affixing the two together to make double-sided paper.

2 Referring to the diagram, *right*, cut out the card shape, using a paper trimmer and crafts knife to make the diagonal cuts. Measure and mark the fold lines on the card stock. Run a scoring tool, held with very little pressure, along the fold lines. Fold the card in thirds.

3 Cut triangles and glue them onto the inside panel with a glue stick. Layer 2 rectangles and adhere with glue stick. Write a message on the rectangle and glue onto the front panel.

4 To make an envelope, see *pages 109–110*. Glue coordinating paper onto the envelope flap.

**1 square = 1 inch
Enlarge at 400%**

cups of cheer

what you'll need

- Heavyweight solid and floral patterned papers
- Vellum paper
- Note cards
- Tracing paper
- Pencil
- Scissors
- Mini brad paper fasteners
- Crafts knife
- Double-stick tape
- Tea and individual serving hot chocolate packages
- Envelopes or paper and tracing paper

here's how

1 Trace the patterns, *page 108;* cut out. Use the patterns to cut out two contrasting paper mugs, teacups, or teapots along with a single matching handle.

2 Stack the pair of cups (or teapots) right side up one over the other. Working on the left side first, slide the top cup to the right to reveal an eighth of an inch of the cup underneath. Use the crafts knife to make an $1/8$-inch slit through both layers of paper at the top and bottom of the cup.

3 Slide a brad fastener through each slit, separate the metal ends, and press them flat against the back of the mug.

4 On the right side of the cup, slide the right edge of the card to the left to reveal the edge of the cup underneath. Position the handle ends over the right edge of the top cup. With the crafts knife make a $1/8$-inch slit through the three layers of paper at the top and bottom of the handle.

5 Thread a brad fastener through each of the slits, and press the metal ends flat against the back of the cup.

6 Slide the tea bag or individual hot chocolate serving into the paper pocket.

7 Decorate the note cards with vellum and patterned paper. Apply double-stick tape to the back of the finished cup to attach it to the front of the decorated card.

8 To make an envelope, see *pages 109–110.*

9 **For the tag,** cut a house shape from paper. Cut a tea label to fit tag. Punch a hole in the corner of the tea label. Thread ribbon through hole. Glue label to tag.

Even when you can't get together, you can share a cup of tea with a dear friend or relative with these paper pocket note cards.

greetings

Come on over for tea.

It's time for a chat with you.

Mug Handle Pattern

Mug Pattern

Teacup and Teapot Handle Pattern

Teacup Pattern

Teapot Pattern

Teapot Pattern

getting your greetings delivered

the envelope

You can purchase envelopes in a variety of colors and sizes in scrapbooking, office supply, and stationery stores. If you wish to make coordinating envelopes to complement your handmade cards, follow these instructions, *below.* Many of the instructions for the cards in this book also include tips for embellishing the envelopes to make them a perfect match.

what you'll need

- A card (to determine envelope size)
- Tracing paper
- Pencil
- A sheet of paper
- Scissors
- Adhesive

here's how

1 On *page 110* are patterns for three sizes of envelopes. If these sizes do not meet the needs of your card, adjust the dimensions as described in Step 2.

2 Enlarge and trace or copy the pattern onto the wrong side of a sheet of paper and cut out. Score along the dashed fold lines. Enlarge or reduce the pattern so that your card fits inside the center area with at least a $1/8$-inch border all around.

3 Fold in the side flaps and apply adhesive to each. Fold up the bottom flap and secure it to the side flaps.

4 For the business and rectangle envelopes, fold in the side flaps and apply adhesive to each. Fold up the bottom flap and secure it to the side flaps.

5 Place the card inside, apply glue to the top flap, and seal.

post office tips

Here are some things to remember before you take your greeting cards to the post office:

- Square envelopes require extra postage. Check with your local post office.

- The thickness of the envelope (with the card inside) must be between .007 inch and $1/4$ inch. Envelopes must be between $3^{1}/_{2}$ inches and $6^{1}/_{8}$ inches high, and between 5 inches and $11^{1}/_{2}$ inches long.

- To make an envelope, use a heavyweight paper that is lighter than card stock (which is too stiff to fold). Avoid glossy and dark papers. The print is difficult to read on them, and it is difficult to attach bar codes to them.

- To mail dimensional items, such as the Halloween invitation on *page 52*, consider using boxes, cans, or other items for the container. Check with your local post office to find out what is acceptable and the applicable charges.

- Since the envelope is the "wrap" of your gift, think of the postage stamp as the bow. Check the selection of stamps at the store and use one with an appropriate theme or one that coordinates with the color of the envelope.

special delivery

When the mailing process is eliminated and you decide to hand-deliver a card, there are more options for the outer wrap. Here are creative materials to substitute for a plain paper envelope:

- Handkerchief
- Tissue paper
- Netting
- Fabric
- Cellophane
- Napkin
- Newspaper
- Faux leather

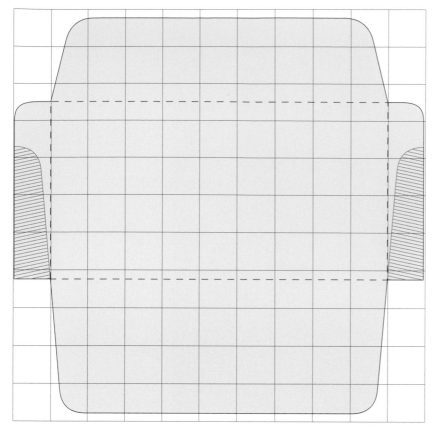

9×4¾-inch envelope
1 square = 1 inch

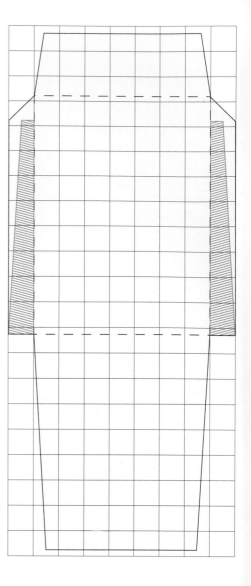

9×7-inch envelope
1 square = 1 inch

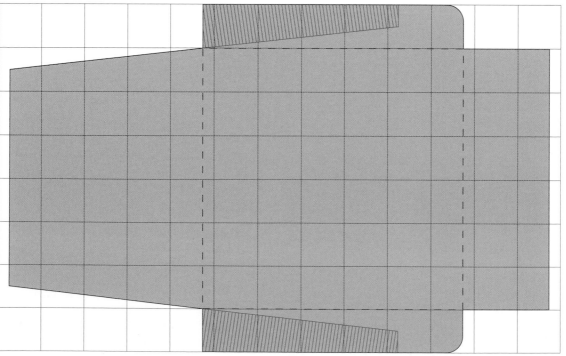

6-inch square envelope
1 square = 1 inch

index

sources & credits

ADHESIVES
Aleenes
duncancrafts.com

Centis
Centis Consumer Products
Division
888/236-8476

Elmer's Glue Stick
800/848-9400
elmers.com
comments@elmers.com

Suze Weinberg Design Studio
732/761-2400
732/761-2410 (fax)
Suzenj@aol.com

Tombow USA
800/835-3232
tombowusa.com

BRADS
Magic Scraps
972/238-1838
magicscraps.com

BUTTONS
Le Bouton Buttons
Blumenthal Lansing Co.
563/538-4211
563/538-4243 (fax)
sales@buttonsplus.com

EYELETS
Persnippity
801/523-3338
persnippity.com

FIBER
Cut-It-Up
530/389-2233
cut-it-up.com

FOAM SQUARES
Therm O Web
800/323-0799

**OPAQUE WRITERS/
WATERPROOF MARKERS**
EK Success Ltd.
eksuccess.com
(Wholesale only. Available at
most crafts stores.)

RUBBER STAMPS/INK PADS
Art Impressions
800/393-2014
artimpressions.com

Stampin' Up!
801/601-5400
stampinup.com

**SCISSORS, PUNCHES,
AND ROUNDERS**
Creative Memories
800/341-5275
creativememories.com

Fiskars Scissors
608/259-1649
fiskars.com

Emagination Crafts, Inc.
866/238-9770
service@emaginationcraftsinc.com

EK Success Ltd.
eksuccess.com
(Wholesale only. Available at
most crafts stores.)

SCRAPBOOK PAPERS
All My Memories
888/553-1998

Anna Griffin
404/817-8170 (phone)
404/817-0590 (fax)
annagriffin.com

Art Accents
360/733-8989
artaccents.net

Bazzill Basics Paper
480/558-8557
bazzillbasics.com

Colorbök
800/366-4660
colorbok.com

Daisy D's Paper Co.
801/447-8955
daisydspaper.com

DMD, Inc.
800/805-9890

Doodlebug
801/966-9952

Family Archives
888/622-6556
heritagescrapbooks.com

Frances Meyer, Inc.
800/372-6237
francesmeyer.com

Hot Off The Press, Inc.
800/227-9595
paperpizazz.com

Karen Foster Design, Inc.
karenfosterdesign.com

Making Memories
800/286-5263
makingmemories.com

Memories Forever
Westrim Crafts
800/727-2727
westrimcrafts.com

The Paper Loft
866/254-1961 (toll free)
paperloft.com
(Wholesale only. Available at
most crafts stores.)

Pixie Press
888/834-2883
pixiepress.com

Plaid Enterprises, Inc.
800/842-4197
plaidonline.com

Provo Craft
provocraft.com
(Wholesale only. Available at
most crafts stores.)

Sandylion
800/387-4215
905/475-0523 (International)
sandylion.com

Scrap-ease What's New, Ltd.
800/272-3874
480/832-2928 (fax)
whatsnewltd.com

Sweetwater
14711 Road 15
Fort Morgan, CO 80701
970/867-4428

Westrim Crafts
800/727-2727

Wübie Prints
wubieprints.com
(Wholesale only. Available at
most crafts stores.)

Two Busy Moms
800/272-4794
TwoBusyMoms.com

STICKERS
Canson
800/628-9283
canson-us.com

Highsmith
800/558-3899
highsmith.com

K & Co.
816/389-4150
KandCompany.com

me & my BIG ideas
949/589-4607
meandmybigideas.com

Once Upon A Scribble
702/896-2181
onceuponascribble.com

Paper Punch
800/397-2737

Paper House Productions
800/255-7316
paperhouseproductions.com

SRM Press
800/323-9589
srmpress.com
(Wholesale only. Available at
most crafts stores.)

Stickopotamus
P.O. Box 1047
Clifton, NJ 07014-1047
973/594-0540 (fax)
stickopotamus.com

**RUB-ON LETTERING
AND MOTIFS**
Chartpak, Inc.
800/628-1910
800/762-7918 (fax)
chartpak.com

The Paper Patch
www.paperpatch.com
(Wholesale only. Available at
most crafts stores.)

DESIGNERS
Susan Banker
Heidi Boyd
Tom Conway
Carol Dahlstrom
Dena Swartslander
Alice Wetzel

PHOTOSTYLING
Carol Dahlstrom
Donna Chesnut, assistant